TABLE OF CONTENTS

Me Myself & I
Soul'd Out

CHARESE NICOLE MATTHEWS

ISBN: 0692792597
ISBN 13: 9780692792599

INTRODUCTION

"Yes, God, I hear you...I'm up." Those were the words I quietly whispered, struggling to open my eyes and make sense of—or should I say put in order—the words that were coming to me while asleep. It was clear that I wasn't dreaming. After consciously trying several times to make myself go back to sleep, I settled with the notion that something of great benefit was about to take place... Yet I continued to lay.

Tossing and turning, I yawned and even yearned to go back to sleep. However, there was this persistent yet gentle nudge in my spirit, followed by a still small voice. This download of potent information had to be completed. It had to be in response to one of the many questions lingering in my unsettled spirit. Or maybe it would simply be words of hope, truth and or encouragement to help maintain my daily sanity.

The words were clear, and the message was strong. I realized immediately that the time was now to move forward. And my excitement began to grow, as I kept mentally repeating what was so unmistakably spoken. I quickly sat up on the edge of my bed and graciously smiled, as if I had just been bestowed a secret from my best friend. And with a grateful heart, the child-like and quiet response from my lips were the words, "Thank you, God." Yes, He had just answered my prayer!

After waiting, wondering and praying about how I should introduce this book, He had finally confirmed what I already knew. I then felt so humbled and happy to have a personal connection with the Almighty One who has all of the answers to life, as we know it. Whether trivial or complex, hard or easy, His greatness is consistently shown in how He has it all figured out. And it doesn't take Him long to help us figure it out. He hears our prayers and sees our potential snares but is always available to show us how much He cares. If we would only be in position, ready to hear and respond at all times to what He is saying... That alone would save us the time and energy we tend to waste trying to figure out on our own what seems so unclear. It's really simple: pray, expect an answer, pay attention, listen, wake up and do.

We often make life more difficult than it has to be, especially when desiring answers to major questions. Never underestimate how the message of direction comes to you. When you ask in prayer, continue to seek and knock: you will get the answer. Before my answer came on July 5th, I happened to be on social media reading all of the Happy 4th of July posts the day prior. There were uplifting quotes, historical posts, even thoughts from a spiritual perspective as well as pictures of people enjoying family cookouts, picnics and beautiful fireworks. The vibration and energy felt on my newsfeed shouted, "FREEDOM!" How exciting it was to feel everyone's energy! As I continued scrolling, I noticed this one post which read, "Happy Forth everyone." Noticing the misspelled word, a critical thought then came to my mind.

With frowned face and turned-up lip, my eyebrow became slightly lifted as I shook my head and even rolled my eyes. Yes, I was just that displeased by someone not taking the time to do a simple spellcheck before posting their well wishes. I gave the message in the post with the misspelled word no time to penetrate my mind: it was instantly rejected and dismissed. But after taking the time to consciously listen within to my spirit, I heard the same small voice that would awaken me the next morning clearly say, "This message is for you: today is the beginning of your moving forward."

I felt apologetic but grateful that I was open to quickly dismiss the negative thought of criticism I initially entertained. Now clearly inclined to fully receive and embrace the message in the post with the misspelled word, I chose that day to move forward. I even responded in the comment section of the post with a simple, "Thank you." See how God used something as small as a misspelled word to bring me a greater message that would result in my independence and freedom? That post opened in me the free-flowing creativity to accomplish what was before me and to move forward. And, as a result of my obedience, look at how the introduction to this book has flowed.

Perhaps this will be the starting point of your own forward movement. Allow all you have deemed impossible for most of your life to now become possible. Let it become your reality! Open yourself to receive the message God has been trying to get to you for a while now. Claim your independence today! It all begins with your perception: that alone will change your situation. It is ultimately your mind that changes your reality and creates your destiny, so be conscious of your thoughts. Be open to the message, whether it be packaged with or without impressive credentials. See yourself as a receptor of good news and bountiful blessings on a journey toward the desired destiny you've been praying for!

The perception of my reality is simple: I am a woman who loves. I love my Creator, I love life, I love my husband and children, I love peace, I love giving and I love sharing because I express this love. Although life comes with challenges, I consciously make an effort to stay consistent with love. My standard, which I highly regard, is found in the New Testament scripture found in 1 Corinthians 13:4-8. I am building my life on the foundation and principle of love. Having searched for love in many people and things, I have never found any of them capable of meeting the standards outlined in 1 Corinthians 13:4-8. Most importantly, I have had to realize my own failed attempts to meet those standards. And before I could ever test others against them, I had to figure out for myself: (1) How can I apply these Biblical principles to me, and (2) what impact do I need them to make in my life?

As you can see, before this book could even be written, I had to first become my own soul coach! Instead of waiting to hear responses from others, I asked myself those two important questions. I made up my mind to stop overlooking the valuable treasure within and start digging deeper within. As your soul coach, I want to likewise help you discover your own potential as well as gain a deeper revelation of who you truly are—the "you" without the accolades, the approval of others, the pats on the back and the encouragement from friends and family. I want you to know that without all of that—YES! —you still rock! Reading this book is going to help you finally discover the best encourager, coach and support system available: Y-O-U.

So welcome to the journey of your life through the perspective of your soul. You will visit a few memorable places, relive to forgive some other places, rediscover the deserted places and understand the importance of traveling and staying in your own lane. Don't worry: I will be right here with you... But this book is about you and for you... Welcome to your world!

1

SOLDIER – SOUL'DIER

"You don't stop being a soldier because you got wounded in battle"

I love this quote. It has helped me understand my position as a soul coach and soldier. Serving in the army of the Kingdom of Heaven, I am one who helps people gain salvation for their souls, consciousness in their minds, and healing in their emotions. I am one who prays for peace but understands there is a war for the soul. In his farewell speech to West Point, General Douglas MacArthur is quoted as having said, "The soldier above all others prays for peace, for it is the soldier who must suffer and bear the deepest wounds and scars of war." Not only is this my purpose in life, it is what I am most passionate about. Although I have experienced the deepest wounds and scars as part of my own personal soul's war, it has not stopped me from being the soldier that I am. It has actually pushed me even further into my life's calling. Galatians 6:2 reads, "Carry each other's burdens, and in this way you will fulfill the law of Christ" (New International Version). It is my duty as a servant-soldier to serve in this army by bearing the burdens of wounded souls and assisting them in the process of achieving peace, healing and victory!

Have you ever had to come face-to-face with a recruiter, more specifically a military recruiter? I have; and I will just say, if a good friend of mine had not been with me that day, I would have most likely signed up to join the military. At the time, I felt there was nothing to lose! I was young and ready to travel the world. I even thought about how my college tuition would be paid! The recruiter skillfully presented this irresistible package; but the whole time he talked, it was never in my heart to enlist for the reason most soldiers consider—for the love of their country. For me, it was all about the benefits and how promising my future would look, thanks to the prestige and high honors military service would bring. It was not until my girlfriend nudged me and said, "Girl, are you crazy?! You have to go to boot camp!" And, of course, we giggled at the very thought of me going there because I was in no way "a boot camp kind of girl." I neglected to consider the process because all I heard was the promise!

When you choose to enlist, boot camp is a promised part of the military's process of making you a solider. After enlisting, you are given a scheduled ship out date to complete basic combat training and learn the ins and outs of being a soldier. Although I never enlisted in the U.S. military, I have found myself going through another type of boot camp after I told the Kingdom of Heaven, "Yes." I had to discipline myself and put my whole heart, mind and soul into this training. In order to become the SOUL'dier, I had to endure a spiritual, soul-seeking boot camp that took me through trial and error, pain and problems, wrong beliefs and even physical beatings! (NOTE: Throughout this book, you will hear me refer to "soldier" as "soul'dier" because it takes a committed, disciplined soul to go through boot camp and obtain that which is necessary for survival during times of war.) Yes, my past was full of defeat and let downs; but through it all, I am a Soul-Survivor! As a result of my boot camp experience, I recognized the strength and power I had within to change and become the Soul'dier I am today... And this book has been written to declare that you also have this same strength and power!

Here is my question to you: have you yet recognized enough strength in you to enlist? Are you tired of experiencing life defeated in the battle of your mind? I promise, you will not hear me say all those beautiful things the young military recruiter told me. There will be no leaving out the rigors of boot camp, its early morning risings, the discipline it requires, even the battles and wars to be fought after completing basic training. Yes, all those challenges accompany the fabulous benefits. My desire is that you enlist because you love yourself enough to fight for yourself, each day determined to fight the good fight of faith. It's then that all of the fabulous benefits will follow, along with self-actualized "value" and prestige. Just as a good soldier fights for the love of his/her country, a good Soul'dier fights to live a fulfilled life!

So, since you are still reading this book, I think we can safely agree that you have been recruited to enlist. Congratulations! You're now in and on your way from being a sojourner to becoming a "soul'dier". Welcome to the ranks! Your life story is about to change... Up until now, your story may have been that you already completed basic combat training or, at the very least, have some knowledge of it. Although you have probably experienced the battles of life, you are still functioning despite a few internal bruises. Or perhaps you daily grapple with the effects of war, such as flashbacks, memory lapses or sometimes reverting back to old pains through which you suffered and endured. You might even be the one who simply surrendered—throwing in the towel or waving a white flag—in response to being terribly wounded and defeated. To ensure your survival, it probably made more sense to just surrender and comply with your enemy's demands. And I dare not fail to mention the many casualties of war. Perhaps your story has you feeling lifeless, like those whose battles ended by assassination in the combat zone. Even if you feel like an emotional casualty of war, be encouraged: you're physically still alive. Despite how you feel right now, understand that feelings are inconsistent and have the ability to change. And as a result of reading this book, I believe you will change.

Yes, the boot camp process gets tiring and takes a toll on the emotions; however, my advice to you is, "Hang in there, don't lose the battle!" What a shame it would be to lose a battle that you have complete control over! Basic combat training requires you to know your enemy and get properly equipped for battle. As part of this process, you are being issued all of the grenades and ammunition necessary to win! And when you know that you are on the winning the team, there are no losses! As a soul'dier, you can't lose when you know the battlefield and the strategies of your attacker, the very assassin of your soul! Furthermore, knowing your God, your strength, your power and yourself will ensure you fight with confidence, which is something life experiences may have you low on right now. But we are going to deal with that, too.

When soldiers undergo basic training, they are being expertly trained to serve and protect. Recruits begin the process as civilians and must be trained to think and act differently, having a completely different disposition than that of normal citizens. Even their perspective and mentality about the country they serve differs from those citizens who have not served in the military. There is an oath (or soldiers creed) that brings recruits into agreement with the government that esteems them as people of importance. As a result of taking that oath, it now becomes their required duty to fight out of the love they have for their country! And so it must be for you in the fight for your soul...

As long as we are living, there will be an internal war. I am here reminded of what American philosopher George Santayana said: "Only the dead have seen the end of war." What will keep you fighting is the love you have for the wellness of your soul. Yes, love will prevail. It is the driving force for this mission, even its foundation. And in order for the fighter in you to rise up, it will take your soul embracing love and all that it offers. Love must become your standard. In order to uphold this standard, daily examination of your soul is required (i.e. emotional frequency levels, heart issues, mental shifts, and body postures) to ensure you remain in alignment with love and the work it has been sent to accomplish within.

In case you may be asking, "So what exactly is within?" I am referring to the very essence of who you are. You are a spirit, with a living soul, having a human experience. This human experience allows us to function with all five of our senses, responding to life as we've been trained by way of our respective upbringings and/or belief systems. How we respond to life also comes by way of what we feel. If what streams out of a wounded soul is hurt and pain, then those experiences are what we will continue to attract. Lower frequency life experiences do seek to connect with the hurt and pain vibrating within us. This is why we must understand that within the soul exists a powerful energy source: it is a place within us that is infinite, eternal and universal. As this thought-provoking statement shared on the soul (in Denise Linn's book Soul Coaching) reads, "The soul is a source that gives rise to form, yet it is unknowable. It is elusive by its very nature, yet it must be nurtured and cared for. We can intuitively understand what its needs are yet never fathom its depths. It is the substance that links our body and spirit to the greater forces of the universe."

The soul needs to be loved, reassessed, caressed, converted and blessed. It may sound easy, but each step requires full attention from all of your soul's members. Think of a vehicle: in order for it to drive effectively, everything has to work efficiently. Take a moment and imagine in your mind whatever kind of car you desire to own or drive. With the goal of making this as personal and relatable an experience as possible, this car will be the one we use in our illustration.

So let's set the stage...For the purposes of comparison, the engine is like your mind. Your thoughts and beliefs are what ultimately create your destiny. Simply put, without the engine, you are stuck and cannot move. Just imagine driving somewhere and your engine goes out. How then will you get to your desired destination? It may require purchasing a new engine or possibly even a new car.

Your engine is the life of the car, and so is your thinking. If your mind stops, then so do your wheels. They won't move, which means the car is not drivable. This brings us to the tires: they represent your will. The will is that part of you which is driven by whatever force is dominating you at the time. In keeping with the same scenario we just started creating, let's say your car has stopped in an undesirable neighborhood on your way to a very important appointment. You are sitting in the passenger seat, trying to figure out what to do because you must make this meeting. Imagine now how you would feel. What feelings are you experiencing there in the seat of your emotions? That's right! You are indeed seated in your emotions, so we will refer to the passenger seat as the emotions. The emotions usually coincide with the mind's belief system until, of course, it feels something different. So now you have the mental illustration I will be using, as we take our journey together through the soul.

The goal of our journey is to allow love to drive us. As mentioned earlier, love is the greatest and highest standard (according to 1 Corinthians 13). So that means we cannot be successful without it. One of the biggest challenges to letting love drive will be breaking down and rejecting our egos. The ego is like the stop sign (or red light) because it will always have you at a standstill, waiting for seasons (or lights) to change. When it comes to being driven by love, ego is sure to get in the way of you discerning the green light of life. It is impossible to really live--let alone move forward--in the realm of the soul, while holding on to your ego. In other words, ego must go to allow Spirit flow. So, as we make further preparation for forward movement, keep in mind that the Father's love also wants to go along with you on this journey.

2

SOUL SUBMISSION –
SOUL'S- MISSION

*"And thou shalt love the Lord thy God with all thy heart, and with
all thy soul, and with all thy mind, and with all thy strength: this is
the first commandment."*

Mark 12:30 KJV

■ ■ ■

"All the ladies, if you feel me, help me sing it out...

I can't believe I believed everything we had would last
So young and naive for me to think she was from your past
Silly of me to dream of one day having your kids
Love is so blind it feels right when it's wrong"

--"Me, Myself and I"
(as recorded by Beyoncé)

As I flipped through channels on the television, I came across the music
video for this song recorded by the very beautiful and talented Beyoncé.

Its catchy hook—the chorus of this very popular secular song—caught my attention. So I stopped flipping channels to watch and listen intently. To get a full understanding of what Beyoncé was truly saying, I quickly ran to my computer and looked up the song's lyrics.

Once I began reading them, there was an instant connection with the song's message. I related to the feelings of disbelief and betrayal portrayed in Beyoncé's vocal performance as well as her musical interpretation of the great strength and independence women maintain despite those feelings. She artistically delivered all of this in such a way that any woman would be encouraged and convinced to agree with the power of "self". It reminded me of a familiar place of my own that I once knew—a place of hurt and betrayal that was yet full of independence. As I listened, the lyrics pointed toward my condition and state of mind at the time: so naive and blind about the true definition of love, yet too strong of a woman to vulnerably seek out the power of love and how to love myself.

The song lyrics even provided a then-and-now comparison between my thought processes and beliefs. I noticed how my mind had been renewed a few years back from that way of thinking. The amount of growth and maturity experienced since then makes me thankful to God! This time of great reflection and conscious awareness indeed made me happy. It gave confirmation to my spirit and satisfied my soul. It helped me to come to a place of resolve within as to why I could never shake the burden God placed in my heart: to help others come into the knowledge of their authentic selves as well as know the heart's desire of the Father towards them and the insurmountable love He has for them. This has become my soul's mission.

Many have not experienced this unconditional love; and because of this, we end up in love with the feeling of conditional love: as long it meets the required condition, we love. Go with me, as we take a look at the lyrics of the song in verse 1:

> "I can't believe I believed everything we had would last
> So young and naïve for me to think she was from your past
> Silly of me to dream of one day having your kids
> Love is so blind it feels right when its wrong"

Now, allow me to preface my song analysis with this: I am not a Beyoncé basher. In addition to my earlier remarks about her, I have always admired her resilience, gift and artistry. Use of this song's lyrics are strictly in reference to the message and revelation of the content of this book. As we venture further into our journey, I'll share more about how the song title represents the three distinct personalities of the soul. But back to the work at hand.

In Verse 1, it sounds as if she had come to the conclusion that she did not make the best decisions in regard to this particular relationship. She then goes on to explain why those decisions were made. The silliness of being young and naive, she expresses, played a major part in her thinking. She also points out what seemed to be a major letdown: dreaming she would someday have kids with a partner she thought loved her. It obviously came out in the end that the partner was expressing a counterfeit kind of love, which blinded her ability to distinguish it from an authentic love.

QUESTION: Have you ever come to these same conclusions in regard to your own life experiences? Maybe you were in some type of relationship and made decisions that—you know deep down inside—were out of character for you. Those decisions may have even been choices you previously told someone else to never make but somehow found yourself making. Your thoughts were probably something like, "I just can't believe this foolishness happened to me," "I don't know what in the world I was thinking," or "That was so stupid of me to do... How could I even allow that to happen?!" Be honest: does that sound familiar to you? I must admit that—to me—it absolutely does.

After experiencing those thoughts in several relationship instances, I finally came into a knowledge that would ultimately stop the cycle of "I can't believe." It's what inspired me to go through the healing process, to be restored and eventually write this book. What I learned helped me come to the conclusion that—due to my ignorance—all of the repetitive cycles, mistakes and/or mishaps of my life were the direct result of low self-esteem, a lack of confidence, a lack of love, and a corrupted belief system. Because I did not understand the value of my existence, I chose—whether consciously or unconsciously—not to learn valuable life lessons. So no, I cannot and will not fully blame my decisions on being young and naive. Contrary to the suggestion of this song's lyrics, some of those decisions were made when I was much older and even knew better.

Over the years, I began to ask questions about my existence and its value. I started spending more time seeking my life's purpose through prayer, study of the Bible, meditation of the scripture and compiling prophetic utterances spoken to my spirit that affirmed my existence. The Most High revealed to me deeper insights as well as hidden truths in His Word concerning who I am, why some of those decisions were made and how to exercise greater degrees of self-discipline, all to ensure I no longer continue down the wrong path. Even today, I continue to study intensely and intentionally—both spiritually and naturally—to gain more insight into God's expectations of me, His desires for me, and who I am in Him.

Interestingly enough, I have always been intrigued with the study of people. Comprehending the mind, how it works, even the very process of thinking—from both natural and spiritual perspectives—are all things of which I remain curious. Throughout my personal and professional studies, I continuously pray for revelation and deeper understanding of unanswered questions, like: Why do people suffer? Why do they struggle? Why are relationships the way they are? Why do we think the way we think? Why do we repeat cycles? As you can tell, I am a woman seeking to know why. Because I honestly want to know the purpose and meaning of life, I am always praying for the wisdom, knowledge and clarity from the All Knowing One, whom I believe can answer all of my questions. I am confident that, just as in times past, He will yet again reveal the answers to me when I am ready to handle the truth.

Now, I've never been afraid of truth. I was just more so afraid of the truth about me. And it took years for me to finally embrace His truth. What hindered my process was how long it took for me to see that the results of living out my own answers to those questions were less fulfilling and more detrimental to me mentally, emotionally and spiritually.

There were seasons and times in my life that, while I endured personal issues or had those "I can't believe" moments, God would then draw me.

He would nudge me or pull my hearts strings, wanting to reveal the answers to my mind or place them in my heart before I even asked. And the moment I finally accepted His call, I knew it would be life-changing for me. In those trying moments following my acceptance of His call, He would either give me insightful direction to help navigate me through or download a word of hope in my spirit to keep my focus on track.

God already knows that we will one day reach a point of realization that enough recycled living is enough. No more experiencing the same kind of broken relationships and friendships with different people! Reliving the same confusion and pain over and over again eventually gets old. He also knows there will come a time in our lives when we simply just want more out of life. We will have learned the lessons of life and come to a place where nothing matters more than change.

A desired change will then, of course, proceed should you truthfully answer a series of questions revolving around—what I like to call—the triple A's: awakening, awareness and answers. There is a need to ask yourself, how did I get here? Why did I make this or that choice? When did I start feeling like this? Where do I start? What should I do? These are all conscious-driven questions that demand reasoning and change. God is waiting with answers; but He answers in part, meaning He'll give you just the information or revelation needed for that time. In other words, as you seek and trust Him, He speaks and reveals the insight you require to continue moving forward.

These questions were all asked when I knew that it was time for change to happen in my life. I was not looking for a temporary fix but a permanent shift, one that would cause my life to further evolve into His thoughts about me. I love the scripture Jeremiah 29:11-13, the latter portion of which The Message translation reads, "I know what I'm doing. I have it all planned out—plans to take care of you, not abandon you, plans to give you the future you hope for." It is so necessary for you to know the thoughts of God and believe that His way of thinking is the best way for your life. To know, believe and continuously seek with all of your heart; to trust the process, invest in yourself and make the necessary changes along the way will get you closer to your desired destination! As a result of the decision

I made years ago to take this journey, I thank God for all of my experiences (whether good or bad). The decisions, repetitive cycles, rejections, broken relationships and anything else that fueled the fire all ignited the passion as well as birthed a desire within me to make change happen. And now, I am able to share with you, through this book, my experiences—unapologetically! He has entrusted me with what I call "a soul-bondage-breaking message," so others can be liberated. This message dissects the thoughts and even challenges beliefs and actions. Intended to bring you into a God-conscious awareness, this message is being shared to motivate you, pump you up, ignite a passion in you, give you hope, plant a seed, do whatever it can to help you see yourself through the eyes of God. I truly believe this book is for everyone; and I am confident that the Father has something in here for you, wherever you are in life.

Everything in this book has changed my life. Writing this is literally my testimony of the power of God! It was no seven-step program to freedom, neither did I beg God to just simply help me. I instead came to a realization that my tears were not going to change my situation. If change was going to happen for me, then I would have to do something different; and the first step was to submit my soul. I came to grips with the truth that my soul was not aligned with the real me. I was out of order, out of place and out of control. The reason I could not relate to others was because I couldn't relate to myself. So lost within myself, I was disconnected from my Source of life. My soul needed healing, but it had to submit in order to receive healing.

So you may ask, "What does it mean to submit your soul?" Well, I'd love to share what that means! Submission is defined as the action or fact of accepting or yielding to a superior force or to the will or authority of another person. When you submit your soul, you are making up in your mind that you are humbly surrendering your soul to a Superior force. There are many things or people to which we all have submitted or yielded our souls over time. Whether you have bared all of your soul or simply scattered pieces of it, there is ultimately one superior force or another that drives us. For the sake of this book, I am only referring to one Superior Force—which is Yahweh, our Heavenly Father. Our total being is under the subjection of His will and His way, consenting to His authority and yielding to His process! The submission of your soul indicates your willingness to trust Him to lead and guide you. No matter how you've tried in past times to change "You" (or fix your life), the act of submission says you now acknowledge that true and consistent transformation comes by way of you tapping into the power of God within you, exploring the possibilities, and consciously becoming who you are! Listen: change is good, but being is great!

After submission has taken place, your process can begin. The next step is getting the soul—that is, your mind, will and emotions—to align itself with change and for change. You must take action and consent to (or be willing to) change your mind! It's critical that I say this: belief is everything... Proverbs 23:7 states, "For as [a man] thinks in his heart, so is he...," or as another translation says, "so he becomes." Whatever you think on long enough will eventually play out in your life. Your thoughts about yourself, your perceptions, even your beliefs will come to be just as you have so thought. There's simply no way around it: you have to change your mind!

The process of thinking differently takes daily discipline. But thinking, according to God's way, is meant to become your soul's lifelong mission, thereby ensuring your soul prospers. Your mission is to find out His way of thinking and come to know what He thinks about you. For instance, envision the very best life you can have. If what you envision is great, then can you imagine how much greater it will be when you agree with His thoughts for you? Today, begin to align your thinking with thoughts of God's very best for you. Doing so will initiate the process of allowing His mind to be in you! A daily renewal of the mind will also help you adopt the habit of believing and thinking positively. Coupled with the use of affirmations, through scriptural readings and rehearsing what God has spoken about you, change is sure to manifest within your inner man.

It is vitally important to submit your soul to the One—and only One—who cares for your soul. This is what I refer to as SOUL-mission (i.e. soul + submission). Not only are you submitting your soul; but now, you are establishing your soul's mission statement. Taking this step was particularly life-changing for me. It took off me the pressure of trying to handle the matters of my own heart, of trying to be accepted and even trying to find my own way. I was always trying something, until I just became tired of trying. It was then that my soul bowed down and humbled itself. Without a trace of resistance, I no longer made excuses for my actions. No more trying to justify my reasoning. I instead repented. And as I prayed to God, my request was that He forgive me of trying to control my own soul without His assistance. I also asked if He would take control of my soul and—by His power—properly and divinely heal, mend, deliver and restore it. All of that had to happen in order for me to give Him complete access to my fragmented mind, so my thinking could be aligned with His.

What a beautiful endeavor to willingly give God access to my soul. But let's be clear: the process was excruciating. However, an immediate change followed! I felt renewed, I felt liberated, I felt a new start, I felt different! I felt His love and envisioned a bright future for myself. My initial feeling was hopeful—so hopeful, in fact, that I had totally convinced myself the struggle was over! Yet, what I failed to realize (in the moment I submitted my soul) was that submission itself would now become an internal struggle. For me to yield, to surrender, to humble myself was completely out of the norm for me. But it felt really good—for that moment—to be free! Having experienced so much hurt in times past, I just longed to be happy. So I'm sure you can imagine why the last thing I wanted to experience was this feeling of freedom leaving me. I knew before long that I would once again be confronted with the inconsistency of my soul. You can call it being emotionally challenged, I suppose. Although I was willing to stay liberated, the tug of war within would soon cause my mind and emotions to collide.

Remember the vehicle illustration given in the book's introduction? My mind (the engine) often times thought its way back to doubt, fear and negative thinking. In addition to that, whatever feeling sat in the front passenger seat would eventually take the wheel, as evidenced by my inconsistent emotions. However, on the day of my soul submission as well as in the days following, this was the good news: I was not mentally persuaded to stay in a negative mindset. To me, this was a great start to my new way of thinking. But deep down inside, I still felt a bit of reluctance coming from my emotions. There was still this battle. The mind wanted to challenge the feelings; and the emotions wanted to change the mind, all while my will hung in the balance of forward movement. Yes, amidst all the internal squabbling between the emotions and the mind, my willingness was not strong enough to convince the mind. And although I willed to be positive, somehow negativity managed to slip through. So there was then a constant juggle between the two. On some days, I had to make myself feel great; and on other days, I had to remind myself to think on greatness as long as I could, in an effort to convince the mind to align with the feeling of greatness. As you can imagine, this was very tiring. When you think about a vehicle, it takes all of the vehicle's components working together for it to be safely driven. Every part plays a major role in getting its passengers to their desired destination. And so it is with the soul: every component of the soul must work together for its desired destination to be reached.

Before we move on to the next chapter, I would like you to take a moment to examine where you are in your life. Grab a pen and a sheet of paper. This evaluation is between God and the "Me" within you... We will deal with "Myself" and "I" later. Next, ponder this: Where are you? Can you identify if you are emotionally bankrupt, if you are on an emotional roller coaster, or if you're numb to expressing your emotions? Are you able to tell if you're battling in your mind with negative thoughts, or if you are all over the map just trying to figure life out and where you belong? Would you even know if you are uncertain of who you are and simply need to know your true identity as well as the potential you possess within? This is the time to honestly identify where you are... And don't sugarcoat anything: be completely transparent about it!

Ask yourself if you are ready to submit your soul in one direction. Are you open to consenting and agreeing with the One who can lead you to the pathway of righteousness, soul prosperity and greatness? In order to go down this road, you have to be desperate for change and hungry for it. Better yet, I will venture to say it as the generation of today does: you have to be "thirsty," meaning you will do anything for that something you desire. If you desire change and want to learn how to walk out your life's divine purpose, then get thirsty enough for it. Of course, I can't be the one to change your mind. But I can pump you up, push and—possibly—persuade you... Or at the very least, I can be your biggest cheerleader and encourage you to come on this fantastic voyage of a soul journey. Trust me, you've made the right decision and are headed in the right direction!

Of course, if you just can't seem to get past what you are currently feeling... I would still say this book is definitely for you. However, if you remain unwilling to change, then you should know that unwillingness alone defeats the purpose of you even reading this book. Besides, I strongly and firmly believe you will and can change! Here's my suggestion: simply go back and read this chapter once again to truly get an understanding of what was shared. Sometimes that's all it takes!

Lastly, allow me to say this: you—YES, YOU!!!—have come too far to go back now. You have been traveling the road of life for a while now, and it's time for you to go in the direction of your destiny! I don't know where you are. You may be searching for the key to life, or you may have lost the keys and are frantically searching to find them. Listen: you have nothing else or anything more to lose other than TIME... And time is life. With that being said, it's time you go get your life! Are you ready to join me on this road trip? Well, come on, my friend; and get in the car: let's take a road trip together. There are some things I want to share with you!

3

THE JOURNEY – SOJOURNER

"Trust in the LORD with all thine heart; and lean not unto thine
own understanding.
In all thy ways acknowledge him, and he shall direct thy paths".

KJV Proverbs 3:5-6

Hey, my friend! Thanks for hopping in! Buckle up, take a deep breath and relax: you are in good hands! Before we get on the road, I know you must be wondering, "Where in the world are we going?" But let me suggest another thought. Instead of wondering where we're going, the more poignant question to consider is, "Where in the world have I been?"

I am reminded here of a song back in 1989 by singer Lisa Stansfield, entitled All Around the World. It was about a man and a woman who were in a relationship; and one day, they had a quarrel that went horribly wrong. What started out as a bad argument quickly escalated to a really ugly one. She began to share in the lyrics that there were hurtful words spoken, even alluding to herself as being a "bad" girl after having to admit doing some things he apparently knew nothing about. After spilling the beans on herself, she talked about his response to her awful behavior. He was clearly mad and disappointed; but his reaction—to her surprise—was that he, too, had some hurtful things to say that were never before shared. And as a result of that argument, he left her. In explaining her side of the story, it was clear that she had honestly come to grips with her actions. She took responsibility for the part she played in the relationship dissolving. After admittedly doing too much lying and wasting too much time, she was left there all alone and had been crying since his departure. As she sang about having been around the world and still not being able to find him, she vowed with great determination that she would forever be searching and looking for her baby until she found him.

What a hurtful and horrible way to end a relationship! I loved that song when it was first released, so much so that I couldn't help but wonder if she ever found him. It was real, it was raw! Can you—in any way—relate to this song? Maybe you were like the bad girl in the song; or maybe you had a bad boy, and you really never got closure from this relationship. Some of you would always seem to find yourself searching for or comparing others to this same guy, constantly thinking of him while in other relationships. Yes, as you can see, I have also been here and can definitely relate.

Revisiting my thoughts about the song, I look at it from a different perspective today. While we know she didn't literally travel the world looking for this man, she had most likely moved from relationship to relationship, reliving her past experiences while searching for the one to fill the void or at least help her bring closure to an unsettled soul wound. How did she ever get over him? Or did she just continue going through life attempting to recreate her experience of him with someone else? Another thought to consider: in expressing that she did something horrible and taking the rap for the things she had done to ruin the relationship, did she ever forgive herself? Was she ever healed? Did she ever deal with herself? These are some very important questions that we must get in the habit of posing. So many of us have gone through similar situations and never really took quality time to deal and heal. Just like the woman in the song, we find ourselves here, there and everywhere, searching and searching outwardly instead of searching within ourselves.

Well, we will most likely never know what happened to the character in this song or what journey she took; but I believe this is as good a time as any to talk about where we are going. You may have been on that journey around the world... You may still be traveling and searching for your baby—whatever or whoever that may be. If this is you, then we are changing directions today! This change is necessary for you, and its necessary right now. So, let's talk about the journey!

We are on a mission, a journey through the soul—the very core of our being. We are examining the mind, the will and the emotions, as it relates to Me, Myself and I. However, it is vitally important you keep in mind that a soul without an anchor is a soul out of control. And a soul without an anchor will float on to whatever rocks its boat! In other words, whatever direction satisfies it then dictates the way in which it goes. We cannot truly enjoy the journey of life if unaware of where we are going. Trust me: this journey through the soul will prepare you for the journey of life.

The journey of life—from a Biblical perspective—has two paths, according to Matthew 7:13-14. These two paths lead you to two different destinations. Your path selection is a matter of life and death. One of these paths is most likely to succeed; the other is doomed to fail. These two verses in Matthew 7 are all about the choice between these two paths. They tell us something important about the choice we must make as well as ourselves.

Had the woman in All Around the World explored within herself and discovered why she wanted to search for a man to complete her, she could have very well saved herself a trip around the world. But she instead chose the pathway mostly traveled—that being the one chosen by those who are looking for fulfillment (or even a counterfeit love) in man, money or other material things, all in an attempt to fulfill or cover the void in their soul.

Look at the passage in Matthew 7. Yahushua (Jesus Christ) gives us the opportunity to choose. He gives us a pathway to begin the journey; and although the choice is ours to make, Jesus begins with some wise advice: "Enter through the narrow gate" (Matthew 7:13). Before we even begin to examine the two paths in front of us, Jesus wants us to have the inside scoop: think narrow. "I'm about to give you a choice between two doors. And by the way, if you're paying attention, pick the narrow door." He then gives us a contrast between these two pathways: "...for wide is the gate and broad is the road that leads to destruction, and many enter through it."

The first option is a wide gate and a broad path. The words used here describe a spacious, roomy, expansive highway to travel on. It's just the kind of road you might choose. Travel along this road is easy, and there's ample room to accommodate everyone and all their baggage. This road leads to self-indulgence and eventually destruction, both now and forever; and it should be avoided. Please notice that both of our song examples have taken this road. In Beyoncé's song, Me, Myself and I, the conclusion led us to believe she was headed down Self Road, turning within herself for strength and guidance (with no help from the Most High). She trusted in no other person but herself. Then Example Two wandered around the world with no instruction or guidance, also traveling in search of self-gratification. Can you relate to either of these two examples? I most definitely can. In fact, I can relate to them both. But there is another option!

The road that He has made available to us is the road of Life. Verse 14 states, "But small is the gate and narrow the road that leads to life, and only a few find it." It's not a popular road at all. Think of the back roads in your community that are not traveled frequently and compare them to all of the major highways or the more popular main streets. Traffic is normally backed up on the main roads because everyone has the same idea and thought process.

This reminds me of when I lived in Virginia. My job was literally twenty minutes away; however, traffic was horribly congested every day during rush hour. It was so backed up that what would normally be a twenty-minute trip was more like forty-five minutes to an hour. The quickest, most popular way to my job was to either get on the HOV or take I-95 straightway. Although it seemed quicker, since my exit was only a few exits down, I would somehow still end up late for work. I eventually began to inquire from coworkers about other ways to get to work. Although they suggested multiple roads, highways and streets, it still took me some time to make a decision. Attempting to go another way uncovered a fear of getting lost or simply traveling an unfamiliar path. However, I confronted that fear and chose a path. I made the decision to go; and before long, I had embarked on a wooded, narrow, two-lane road. My start was very cautious and attentive. Since I could not clearly see if other vehicles were coming from the opposite direction, there were certain parts of the road that required extra caution. Nevertheless, the oncoming traffic was minor. By this being the road less traveled, I encountered none of the traffic woes previously experienced and was able to get to work on time.

Many times, people travel the popular roads because of convenience and/or comfort. They are familiar with the road, even knowing how to maneuver in and out of traffic. They'll cut people off to get ahead or do whatever else is necessary to arrive at their destination. Some people will skip the long, drawn out journey altogether and find other ways to cut travel time (i.e. carpooling). They'd rather not involve themselves with traveling down a solemn, lonely and long road. For them, it would feel better jumping on the bandwagon or riding on other's dreams and visions, all the while missing out on what the journey is really all about. My choice, however, was to travel this narrow road. And I decided that during my commute to and from work, it would be a time of solitude, reflection and prayer. It allowed me time to be conscious of my surroundings and more attentive to unexpected events, along with the possibilities of what was to come. Traveling on that road was very peaceful: I was not bogged down with the congested stop-and-go of traffic, neither was I stressed out with trying to beat the time nor panicking over whether or not I would be late to work.

Going back to the Bible passage, we see Jesus describes this narrow road for us. The beginning of the path is restrictive, and narrow is literally "pressed together" (or restricted). The implication is not that of the road being spacious. So yes, it could be hard—at times—to navigate. On this restrictive and narrow road, attempting to get through will be a rather tight squeeze. Pressure Street and Pressing Avenue will be the two side streets that will lead you through those uncertain times of growth and development in your life. You will have moments of persecution and moments of peace. Sometimes you may even feel like wanting to rebel, but repentance will be in your heart. You will face a mountain of depression, but deliverance will intervene to stop what could have turned into a head-on collision.

The narrow road is everything opposite of Self. In fact, traveling this road alone will cause you to confront Self. During your trip, you will come to a self-check point and there find out that self-sacrifice and self-denial are both necessary for the journey. Of course, there are perks and benefits while on this journey: you are divinely led, you have GPS that will give you advance warnings; and you have the privilege of missing out on all of the traffic frustrations and having to switch from lane to lane as well as the pressure of dealing with aggressive drivers and all other forms of related spiritual resistance. All the distractions of the popular road are removed, thereby ensuring your only focus on the narrow road is that of dealing with you!

Now as you travel on this road, you will recognize that there are others also taking this route. However, don't expect to fit in or even be popular on this road: it's a selfless road. This journey is more about Him navigating you, as you explore and site see yourself from His perspective. Until you reach your final destination, the journey is giving you the opportunity to see through God's eyes who you are, what your purpose is and where you are going.

So now that we've got that out of the way, I think we've sat here and talked long enough. Are you buckled up and ready to ride? Good. Hopefully, after thinking about where you have been, your earlier question about where we're going has been answered. Let's hit the road!

Please relax, rest your head and imagine yourself listening to some soothing instrumental music playing softly through the stereo speakers. If you would, create in your mind the image of a beautiful summer day. Think early Saturday morning. It's about seventy-five degrees. The birds are chirping; you look out of the window and admire the peaceful scenery, as you take a deep breath. You feel thankful; and although you are alone, you feel content.

Now imagine this: you have just handled all of your personal business and chores at home, and you feel a sense of accomplishment. You decide to take a road trip; but before doing so, you stop at the service station to make sure all is well with your vehicle. Everything is in order; you're now good to go. And since there's money in your pocket, you get the idea to go splurge on yourself. So you jump in the car and start it up. You're feeling great! With no particular plans or clue of where to go or what to do first, you just begin to drive. And as you are headed down the highway, you sense in your spirit a new beginning—a fresh new start. Your mind begins to wander and think of all the possibilities, all of the dreams you set to the side (due to distractions, such as financial, relationship, or unresolved internal or external issues). This thought holds a special place in your mind, as you began to think of the endless opportunities and possibilities. You then make up in your mind that nothing else will stop you from accomplishing all that you have ever dreamed of. The current feeling of accomplishment has now connected with your thought of accomplishment: both are in total agreement with each other. You are so excited and now start thinking about how to pick up the pieces of your life and finish what you started.

As you are trying to make sense of where and how to begin this process, thoughts of doubt start to rush through your mind: How can I do it? What about time and money? Where do I start? Who will help me? As your thoughts become flooded with all these, you begin pumping the brakes. And by the time you start pondering the last question, both you and the car have been put in park. Clearly, that last question—WHO will help me? —triggered something a little deeper that literally brought your movement to a halt. And as the rabbit trail of thoughts begin again, you sit there in that motionless state thinking—your thoughts anxiously tugging on your emotions for an answer from an unresolved and unhealed soul wound. Your emotions finally muster an answer: "I have no one; no one will support me." And then a whisper reminds you of why you are alone in the first place.

As you can see, the thoughts of doubt can become so overwhelming; they swiftly shift your focus to the impossibilities. It then just becomes way too much for you to even consider changing, because—at this point—your mind and your emotions have shifted directions. But your will struggles to hang on for dear life and quietly says within, "Keep driving, don't turn around." So you listen. In trying to keep that positive vibration going, you get an idea to turn on the radio. That should help dismiss those negative thoughts and clear your mind, right? So, before hitting the power button, you gather your thoughts and—in an attempt to regain control—shake your head, as if to clear the anxiety and negativity from your mind. You take in a deep breath... exhale... turn on the radio... And guess what song is playing? Yep, you guessed right: Me, Myself and I.

Suddenly, you feel different. This feeling of self-independence and self-empowerment, characteristic of the false superwoman of hurt, arises, taking over and dismissing everything you were so desperately trying to fight in your mind just a moment ago. As you begin to sing and agree with the chorus of the song, you settle with the realization it champions and vow to yourself that—at the end of the day—you and only yourself will be in control. After reminiscing about all of the hurt and heartache, you made up in your mind that YOU will govern your own affairs, looking out for you and only you. You have now closed off a part of yourself that no one will ever gain access to again: you have taken complete ownership of yourself. Having "safely" assured yourself that you are all you have at the end of the day, no one else is even suitable to be your best friend. After thinking on these words, daydreaming, and validating your new stance, you come back to reality and notice the radio is still playing... Continuing to be fueled by the song's energy, you join in and co-sign the agreement within your soul by singing,

> Cuz I realized I've got
> me, myself and I that's all I got in the end,
> that's what I found out
> and there ain't no need to cry
> I took a vow that from now on
> I'm gonna be my own best friend.

What a scenario! Has this ever happened to you? Taking a look at this and how it all played out, we could easily conclude the journey has ended. You turned around and—in your feelings—drove back home. You never went any further than your emotions and mind would allow. We could even go to Verses Two and Three of the song, as Beyoncé recounts all of the things she finally realized in this wrong relationship. She allowed her way of thinking and belief system to lead her down pathways that would eventually keep her relying on herself and repeating cycles. We can even look at this from another perspective. Yes, a more optimistic approach would be to at least thank God for allowing you to make it this far. However, despite the fact that you never physically went back to that relationship, you are presently driving into your future stuck—both mentally and emotionally—in the past. The same road is being traveled but without direction this time. In other words, you are wandering in hope that you'll—one day—get to your destination!

There is a journey for everyone to take. Depending on where our soul's perceptions take us or our respective pathways lead, we will all either end up on the winning or losing side of the road! What matters on this journey are our choices… What choices will we make to get to where we want to be? Making better decisions and making this journey with clarity will surely lead us to enjoying greater experiences on the road trip of life.

I can recall taking this one particular road trip with a few of my cousins in my younger years. All we had on our minds was hanging out together, having fun, laughing and heading to New York. We thought through nothing else! No plans were made; no hotel rooms were booked: we just jumped on the road. No thought was given to the possibility of having to either stop on dark roads in unfamiliar small towns or change a flat tire… I'm not even sure any of us had a pager or cell phone to use in case of an emergency. We had one goal: to have fun and get to New York! And by the grace of God, we safely arrived there unharmed.

Unfortunately, some of us are still taking chances. We still have that same mentality of I don't care how I get to my destination, just as long as I have fun all the way. The choices we make are an indication of our maturity and growth. For me, times have changed. My life means more: I am conscious of my choices and love my journey. While I once was a sojourner, that was a temporary mental place for me. Some decisions I made while 19 or 20 years of age would not even be considered today. Besides, planning and setting a goal is much more responsible and leaves little room for the "I can't believe I did or didn't do it" excuse.

To journey simply means to travel from one place to another. Many of us have taken road trip after road trip, journeyed from state to state and traveled from country side to country side by airplane, ship or train. Some trips were just for vacation, to relax and get a break from everyday life. However, others were scouting trips in search of a destination in which to settle and start anew. If not spontaneous, then—in order to really enjoy ourselves—most trips have to be well thought out (i.e. Where do I want to go?), well-planned (i.e. What will I do? Where will I stay?), and financially secure. A great deal of positive energy goes into making sure the geographical location is the best for the occasion, that the type of transportation adequately supports how we make it there; and, of course, that what we plan to accomplish while on the trip is properly arranged.

The same detailed information we collect as well as the time spent ensuring we have planned the best trip in no way compares to the effort most of us put in making our spiritual journey of life the best possible. Often failing to put the same degree of preparation into planning our spiritual journeys, we jump into the vehicle of life with no direction and foolishly spend our money in exchange for so-called happiness or fulfillment, until we find ourselves emotionally, physically and mentally broke. We neglect to take seriously where we end up staying and take on the motel mentality versus that of the favorable five-star one. Mind you, I have nothing against motels; but the point is we do not fully enjoy what God intends for us because we fail to take our spiritual journey as seriously as we should!

Get an understanding that a spiritual journey is simply a journey. And during the journey, there is progression; there is movement. Remember that you are a sojourner; and this place—for you—is only temporary. There is no need for you to travel alone: wisdom, knowledge and maturity are eager to ride along as passengers. Once you accept all that has happened with you up until this point, you should thank God for it—even all that you have deemed unnecessary, painful or difficult to understand. Simply surrender to it. It's okay now. It has brought you to this point in your life, where you must right now yet make another decision to make the best of your circumstances and continue on your journey of exploration.

I am reminded of the African-American abolitionist and women's rights activist Sojourner Truth. She made the decision to escape slavery, along with her daughter, to freedom. I admire her resilience and inward freedom, despite all she endured as a slave. Regardless of what her environment or circumstances were, she understood her freedom in the midst of slavery. She fought a winning battle for us all because she made a decision to see the end result. She had a plan and led the way. She explored. Conscious of the world in which she lived, she understood her "why"—that is, her soul's mission and purpose. She also knew that enemies were all around her and was once even noted as saying she would not allow her life's light to be determined by the darkness around her. Although aware that her life was being threatened and could possibly be taken, her souls perspective on it all can be found in this quote: "I am not going to die, I'm going home like a shooting star." She was light, and her works are still seen in many women today. Sojourner Truth planned to leave a legacy, defending and fighting for the rights of women. She indeed went from a sojourner to soldier! And you, too, are now on your way to doing the same...

If you will, rewind your imagination back to the beginning once more... You have taken your care to be serviced again at the same station, and right before your eyes there are two identical cars with their headlights staring at you. You know that one of them belongs to you and has just been worked on, but you are uncertain which one is yours. Which one do you need to get in? Of course, the easiest way to figure out would be by asking the service mechanic, since he just worked on it. Rather than getting into both cars to see which one your key fits, why not ask? In our lives, we are sometimes uncertain of what really belongs to us. We have been conditioned to see things one way. We look in the mirror and see the outer shell, such as our features. We then get locked into the perspective of only seeing what satisfies us about our appearances. We never realize that which is unique about ourselves, that which separates us from others.

And guess what? We will never know until we first ask our Designer and look closely within to identify who we are and what belongs to us!

So back to our scenario: what would you do? Would you ask the mechanic and let him show you? Or would you take matters into your own hands? WAIT! Before you answer, ponder the questions for a minute. Take a deep breath and let it out. Let's keep riding...

4

IDENTITY – SHOW & TELL ME

"Therefore, if anyone is in Christ, he is a new creation; the old has gone, the new has come!"

2 Corinthians 5:17 (New International Version)

Okay, before continuing, let's stop here and get a cold drink or maybe a cup of coffee or tea—whichever you prefer. I personally prefer coffee. Alright, are you ready to talk some more? In the last chapter, I asked you to wait and ponder the question—What would you do? —before answering. Would you ask the mechanic and let him show you, or would you take matters into your own hands? I asked you to wait because, in addition to the two identical cars, I want you to look at something else. First, I'd like for you to act as if you are pulling out your imaginary keys. Next, take a good look at them. Imagine that the service man gave you two sets of keys and you had to decipher which set belongs to you. Although it is possible for you to not be able to identify the car right away, you will definitely know what key chain belongs to you.

When in the process of car shopping, you may already know the make and model of vehicle you want. And although the dealership has many vehicles of the same make, model and year, what differentiates each vehicle is its key cut and unique vehicle identification number. But once a car is purchased a car, it's normal to add a key chain to the car key to properly identify or personalize it. We can look at this key from a spiritual perspective. Everyone is given the key to life. Let's call it potential. The key is designed to fit the ignition of a vehicle specifically for you.

We, as children of the Most High, are created in His image and likeness. We serve a purpose for Him and have all been given potential and a measure of faith to make the best out of the life He has freely given to us. But what sets you apart from other people? What have you added to the key that identifies you? Is it a key chain that links to bondage? Or how about fear? Maybe it's linked to abandonment or rejection? Or have you yet realized that the key in your possession can potentially get you in the right car and on the road to success, allowing you to experience love, peace and prosperity?

Maybe you have realized your potential but lack motivation or inspiration to put it in the ignition or tap into it? Many of us know we are great but are afraid of our greatness. Many of us know that we have the power of potential, but we somehow still seem to sabotage our efforts. Many of us are running on full but have a slow leak in our exhaust pipe. And so my questions to you are, "Where is your potential? What ignites you? What starts your engine?"

As simple and funny as it may seem, a change of hair color or a new haircut would have given me the push I needed to feel like I was somebody. It was something tangible, like a new car, that jumpstarted me and made my nobody-feeling-self seem as if I was somebody. My energy source was external, superficial and without substance because I honestly had no fuel. I had nothing to go on. I lacked knowledge of myself and my identity. But I always had my "self-starter kit" ready to revert back and reinvent myself just to continue on in life as somebody. I found this quote from the late actress Sarah Jones quite interesting:

"To what extent do we self-construct, do we self-invent? How do we self-identify? Like, what if one could be anyone at any time? Well, my characters, like the ones in my shows, allow me to play with the spaces between those questions."

In other words, we will continue to live in the realm of somebody, nobody, ANYBODY... To be accepted, we have to be somebody, even when we feel like nobody; but it's okay, because we can turn into anybody! What a great way to live, huh? Of course not! Oh, how I wish I could deal with that a little more. But my point is this: we will continue to self-construct and self-invent when our soul has no confidence within itself. You may ask, "How can the soul have confidence?" The soul has confidence when it is able to identify that it belongs to something greater than itself. It needs to feel connected, it needs to feel safe and secure, and it needs to have a sacred place to call home. And as we previously mentioned, the soul has to serve out its passion and mission. The soul has a purpose. It is always searching for the key to greater awareness, and that is through the key of potential.

"Understanding" is the key which leads us to purpose, and it is available to us all. But it is up to you to decipher what you deem important enough to be understood. As I faced this decision throughout my life, it was not always my choice to be understanding. However, one day--after making the same turns down the same streets and just driving aimlessly--I decided to get an understanding of my life and the purpose for my life. I turned off the radio--with its songs of independence and false freedom--and really wanted to know, "Who is this new person that keeps emerging behind the wheel? Where did she come from? What is the driving force of energy behind this engine? What happened to the vulnerable, willing person ready for change?"

I had questions! And I needed to understand because I had no understanding. Have you ever been down this road? What an overwhelming, tiresome, lonely and frustrating, bumpy road. Are you struggling with this now? The battle is indeed real!

Anytime there is a lack of understanding, there exists a mental war within the soul (i.e. the mind, will and emotions). Each member will never fully agree. In fact, they will all do what they are designed to do, think or feel, in whatever way they think or feel at the time, which results in inconsistency and frustration. Internal confliction of the soul will seldom allow the authenticity of the spirit of God to consume and caress the soul with a divine awareness of identity, truth and understanding. Of course, this only happens when the will is not strong enough to convince the mind and emotions to embrace God. Such denial of awareness results in a superficial connection to a false identity rather than a supernatural division of soul and spirit.

When faced with a sudden decision to change or not, the Spirit is always willing to change. He is rooting for you to tap into the true reality of who you are, but the ego of a wounded soul will join forces together to create a face that will cover up or hush the confusion within. The book of Romans testifies of this confusion or war within. YOU MUST read this passage! I chose the Message Bible translation, as it captures the contextual spirit of the scripture and helps us grasp a greater understanding of what the Apostle Paul is going through. Take notice of all that it highlights.

Romans 7:14-16 (MSG) I can anticipate the response that is coming: "I know that all God's commands are spiritual, but I'm not. Isn't this also your experience?" Yes. I'm full of myself—after all, I've spent a long time in sin's prison. What I don't understand about myself is that I decide one way, but then I act another, doing things I absolutely despise. So if I can't be trusted to figure out what is best for myself and then do it, it becomes obvious that God's command is necessary.

17-20 But I need something more! For if I know the law but still can't keep it, and if the power of sin within me keeps sabotaging my best intentions, I obviously need help! I realize that I don't have what it takes. I can will it, but I can't do it. I decide to do good, but I don't really do it; I decide not to do bad, but then I do it anyway. My decisions, such as they are, don't result in actions. Something has gone wrong deep within me and gets the better of me every time.

21-23 It happens so regularly that it's predictable. The moment I decide to do good, sin is there to trip me up. I truly delight in God's commands, but it's pretty obvious that not all of me joins in that delight. Parts of me covertly rebel, and just when I least expect it, they take charge.

24 I've tried everything and nothing helps. I'm at the end of my rope. Is there no one who can do anything for me? Isn't that the real question?"

Boy, how powerful and prophetic this scripture is when it comes to explaining the war between Me, Myself and I!

The conflict indicates that there is always a battle between the two identities within, which are the Self (soul) and the identity we have in Christ (spirit). There is always a war for influence between good and evil. We are always in battle to make decisions that will either confine us to our limitations or compel us to move toward greater exploits and more fruitful experiences. God desires for you to come in to this knowledge: there is so much more for your life than hurt, pain and self-absorption.

Remember when you were on the imaginary road trip in Chapter 1? You sensed a new beginning. You felt that something different needed to happen in your life. You felt change! In that moment, you were experiencing an invitation, a drawing, a spiritual luring to come closer to Him. It was literally a breath of fresh air! The wind of God was gently blowing you in His direction, while tapping on the door of your heart. What quickly followed that drawing was the eruption of mental distraction, which took your focus. And one of your senses alerted you of this distraction, so you breathed back in the smell of your reality and tuned in to the frequency of what was familiar to your soul. The possibilities of what could be new were quickly snuffed out; and the wall of Self now stands in your way, blocking the "new". When Self is present, it aborts spiritual flow and growth. It limits you to that which you are familiar and comfortable. When you are limited to the desires of your own soul, it takes away your seat in heavenly places. In other words, according to scripture, you cannot be seated in heavenly places standing in a soulish realm. The passage below taken from Ephesians 2:1-8 (The Message Bible) clearly confirms how the Father wants to bring us into a higher level of consciousness concerning who we really are in Him. By allowing us to be seated in Heavenly places, we see ourselves as He sees us! He gives us clarity as well as access to His mind and all that He desires for us. But the wall of Self and the stagnated life polluted with unbelief keep us living as underprivileged children wandering on the road of life. Once again, take notice of the highlighted words.

Ephesians 2:1-6 (MSG) It wasn't so long ago that you were mired in that old stagnant life of sin. You let the world, which doesn't know the first thing about living, tell you how to live. You filled your lungs with polluted unbelief, and then exhaled disobedience. We all did it, all of us doing what we felt like doing, when we felt like doing it, all of us in the same boat. It's a wonder God didn't lose his temper and do away with the whole lot of us. Instead, immense in mercy and with an incredible love, he embraced us. He took our sin-dead lives and made us alive in Christ. He did all this on his own, with no help from us! Then he picked us up and set us down in highest heaven in company with Jesus, our Messiah.

When we look closely at the scripture in Romans 7, where the Apostle Paul talks about the flesh, he is referring to Self, the sinful Adamic nature that we all were born into. The flesh (or Self) derives from the soul (the emotions, mind and will). According to Webster's dictionary, it is believed to be separate from the body and is the source of a person's emotional, spiritual and moral nature. When Self wins the internal war between the two identities, Satan--the enemy of our soul--works to entangle his desires with your Self's desires. This is done to ensure that you never come into your true identity. AHH!!! IDENTITY!!! This is the trick: he has tried to keep our identity from us for far too long, using people, places or things to bind us to hurtful events, traumatic experiences or to simply keep us living "in our feelings." We have been bound with key tags and chains of despair, despondency and defeat that will not allow us to know our own identity potential!

Think now about something terrible, traumatic or life-threatening that has happened to you, whether in your childhood, some other part of your past or your present experiences. Just think of one thing... Name it and go through the details in your mind. What emotion surfaced from your initial thought about it? Be honest with yourself! Now think of your relationship with the person who caused that pain. Is it a healthy relation-ship at this present date? Have you forgiven them? Are you healed from the memory of it? How does it make you feel today? Again, be honest with yourself!

ME MYSELF & I   35

Honesty within is so important to your identity. We've heard the phrase before to, "Be true to yourself." This is extremely important! Why? Because when we lie to ourselves and deny feelings that are actually there, we then build our own selves up on a foundation of lies and deception. We will lie to ourselves and say, "I am strong," "I don't need him/her or them," "I am over it," or "It doesn't hurt..." NO! Stop it: it's a lie! You are deceiving yourself. God has made us to relate to others, to fellowship with one another. So, don't lie about NOT being hurt! It does hurt that they have rejected me, it hurts that he/she left me, it hurts that I have lost loved ones, it hurts... fill in the blank... Yes, it hurts. Scream it out: "It hurts!!!"

Admitting your hurts does not devalue you. In fact, it speaks volumes! It speaks that you are not the superwoman or superman you have created yourself out to be. It speaks that, in your weakness, you are open to have His strength make you strong! It also gives hope in knowing that you don't have to live your life under the government of Self and its rules, regulations and conditions! It disconnects you from the deception of the enemy, which will attempt to bind you to the feelings of that experience. For instance, if you suffer with low self-esteem, then everything you do, say or think is below the standard of living that you can enjoy.

The war within is real! You are not what you have been through! You are not what they have said about you! You are not your current circumstances! You are not your pain! Many have lost their minds because they could not win the identity war within. Many have embraced various lifestyles because their souls had been tormented with suggestive thoughts, lies and belief systems until they accepted and embraced them as their reality. But God is calling you to come out of multiple personalities, alter ego lifestyles, and identity crises to simply become one with Him, as He reveals who you are and your identity in Him!

Identity theft is a serious matter! The Self that agrees with itself and sows into itself will only reap from and for itself, which inhibits growth, progression, wholeness and healthy relationships. However, when Self comes into a place where it needs more than itself, it needs evaluation and stimulation. And to be better, it realizes that it's in need of the Spirit of God. Once it starts to sow into the things of God, then will it reap bountifully from God!

When your identity is stolen from you by way of embracing lies, validating unkind words and not knowing who you are, the enemy loves it and desires to keep you in confusion. You have lost your true self! Think back to the two identical cars in the last chapter that are facing you. Bewildered and confused as to which car you need to get into, you stand there looking... It's not until you actually get in, look around and test it with the key that you correctly identify which car is yours. So it is with you! Things have happened in your life that have left you standing confused. You have no clue, you lack understanding. And although you have created a carbon copy image of what you desire to be or how you would like your life to go, you go back and forth: you don't know which way to go, which car to get in, or which road will get you to your destination. Confusion is what that sounds like to me. And it is all due to loss of identity and lack of understanding.

The key in your hand is to life, but you must first understand that your ultimate goal is to become aware of the power you possess within. You have potential with power! Proverbs 28:5 says, "they that seek the Lord understand all things" (KJV). Understanding gives insight and clarity while you are journeying through life. It also reveals purpose to your existence. The more you understand purpose, the more you become conscious of your true self in Him! Proverbs 4:7 also states, "with all thy getting [of wisdom] get understanding" (KJV). Incline your heart to it, lift your voice for understanding: it provides you with opportunity to discern the sayings of understanding, acquire wise counsel and make better decisions. "For wisdom will enter into your heart, and knowledge will be pleasant to your soul" (Proverbs 2:10 NASB). Did you read that? Let me say it again... Knowledge will be pleasant to your soul... Knowing what you need brings pleasure to your mind, will and emotions! Not only that, but as Proverbs 2:11 continues, "Discretion will guard you, Understanding will watch over you" (NASB). WOW! Isn't it good to know you can prevent repeating the same cycle, traveling the same crowded yet lonely road, and limit your "I can't believe moments" (like in the song "Me, Myself and I"), if you took the key of understanding and applied it to your life? Decisions will no longer be made from a lack of understanding and from the inconsistency of a false identity. God makes it very clear: you cannot help but to know your identity when you are connected to the One who knows YOU best, your Creator.

5

ME – THE SHOW OUT

"Create in ME a clean heart, O God; and re-
new a right spirit within Me."

Psalm 51:10

There is a lot to be covered during the ride as it relates to the soul. The soul – as we have covered - is the very core of your being, it is your mind, will and your emotions. With this understanding, we realize how important it is to submit your soul to God who desires to lead and guide you (like a GPS or compass) through the journey of life. He also desires for you to come into greater knowledge of your identity and your purpose, before you get into the vehicle that He has designed for you. As you know, before taking a road trip, it is important to have instructions and directions for your final destination. Just as, or even more importantly, is the key which unlocks understanding, wisdom and knowledge. All of these combined, give us the assurance that the journey will be successful. No one wants to jump into a car and waste gas or time riding in circles without knowing where they are going. Right? Right!

I know it's a bit much to chew on, but take your time; digest and medi-tate on what was fed to your spirit. Hopefully your appetite has become insatiable. Let's look at it like this; if we were driving along and decided we wanted to get something to eat, perhaps we would pull into a fast food place. I'd invite you to get whatever you would like to eat. I order the three in one combo meal.   Hmm, three in one? In the context that the three in one is generally used, it would mean that one product (or device) has three functions. In the context of this book we are talking about Me, Myself and I, which are synonymous to the mind, will and emotions - three functions of the soul. For the sake of the book, let's just say we are a combo, mind, will and emotions, plus me, myself and I. Many of us work from and live out all three functions as one; this three-in-one person is considered whole! But then we have those who are dysfunctional. The three compartments of the soul are imbalanced, unequal, and fractured. One is leading the others, or possibly at different times the others are dominant, similar to being bipolar.

'It's like everyone tells a story about themselves inside their own head. Always. All the time. That story makes you what you are. We build ourselves out of that story." Patrick Rothfuss, the Name of the wind (The Kingkiller Chronicle, #1)

Let's start with "ME". Me is who we embrace. "Me" is who we want others to see. - "Me" is the show out (a term used when someone wants to be seen or needs extra attention). When we look at it from a grammatical viewpoint, me is a first person pronoun, the objective case of the pronoun I. In school we were taught that the object of a verb receives an action in a sentence. For example: She gave me instructions.   "ME" receives the instruction from "She." Me is the object, or the center of attention. Me is our introduction to the world, the show off; the one we best identify with based on how we feel, or how we look at the time. In this book "ME" symbolizes the emotions.   Normally we act out of how we feel, and synchronize with that feeling. Me is the ideal person that we eventually want to become even if we truly don't see ourselves that way. We can walk the walk, talk the talk, and yet be far from the truth of who we represent. In most cases ME is the mask of the soul.   Have you ever stared in the mirror for a long time and questioned who you really are? I can recall looking in the mirror after I have made up my face, combed my hair and prepped myself and once I've done it all, I stare at my image with this thought in my mind, "I really wish I felt like I look". It is in that moment I look beyond the surface into my hurting soul and saw a different woman. I saw pain, I saw low self-esteem, and I saw rejection and abandonment.

I did not really know who the real Me was, in fact I was staring at someone I had created to impress the world, to please others, to fit the character I desired to be, or to be socially accepted. I felt so far detached from the other half of my soul. I knew I needed to understand MYSELF more and figure out what was separating me from who I really am.

Associate Clinical Professor of Psychology at Harvard Medical School and author of "Identifying and Understanding the Narcissistic Personality", Elsa Ronningstam, says "Referring to yourself in the third person creates distance between "I" and "he." So if you have an exaggerated view of how great you are, you could be using this distance to make yourself even bigger. Or, if you've achieved major success suddenly, using the third person could be a way to adjust to the bigger role that's been assigned to you. It's a way to enlarge yourself to fit that role."

There was a huge role that I needed to fit in and play. Instead of "just being" who I am, I created a huge void that needed filling. The space between Myself and I, left ME, out there hanging on, and continually trying to maintain the "role" without the support of my mind and will. The result of this separation - I was led strictly by my emotions. We have seen celebrities in the media who display what a fractured soul can cause. This includes nervous breakdowns, anxiety, depression, suicidal thoughts, loneliness, schizophrenia, illness, and so much more. Although we have been blessed, or fortunate to be privy to many theories, facts, resolutions, and solutions to maintain mental stability and health, I believe the most critical understanding is – soul matters are a vital spiritual matter. We are spirits, living in a bodies with souls. We are spiritual beings first, and that is the part we fail to acknowledge. We have become accustomed to living as a human seemingly apart from the realm of our soul, which causes us to want and desire the things of the world verses the spiritual things. When the soul is leading the way, our spirit becomes subject to the soul. Although our spirit is willing to function according to the Spirit, it is limited by the expressions of the soul, and whatever issues the soul has, our behavior will reflect it. This is why healing of the soul is necessary. When we experience life from this emotional reality it may seem that whatever comes our way is a personal and direct attack on us causing us to respond in a hurtful, revengeful, spiteful, or negative way. We then become controlling, manipulative and deceitful in our behavior. Our attitude is selfish and vindictive and ripe with a woe-is-me attitude. Everything becomes about "Me". When this happens it is an indication that "I" have taken possession of "my "Self's state or condition based on "Me" (my feelings).

Think about this, when it is just centered on me, as it relates to the combo meal, we have just missed the deal. There is no combo meal deal. Why? Because you get more for your money when you combo it, rather than ordering one item from the dollar menu. In other words, there is more to you than the outer appearance or what you feel. You have more of yourself to offer. Me is only a fraction of the total you!

When I realized that it was Me that needed help, when I realized Me needed to get out of the way, I began to seek out the answers of who I am. I realized that I was really the problem to many of my issues. I had no one else to blame but Me. All of my wrong relationships, decisions and perceptions stemmed from my fractured soul.

My first step was to acknowledge (as the old saints used to sing), "It's me, it's me Oh Lord, standing in the need of prayer, not my mother, not my Father, but it's me Oh Lord standing in the need of prayer." I had become a product of my emotions. I had become one with the feelings. I desperately needed a separation that could only be done divinely.

My second prayer and step was found in the scriptures, Psalms 51. I had a soul wrenching cry out to God to do whatever was necessary to Me and for Me. I acknowledged my sin, my wrongdoings, even as small as creating someone other than what He created me to be. I no longer wanted to be the show out. I wanted Him to hide me, cover me and show me the real me. I wanted nothing hidden from Him nor did I want to Him hide anything from me. I just wanted Him to break me down and build ME. I felt the sentiments of David's heart's cry in the scriptures. "2 Wash me thoroughly from mine iniquity, and cleanse me from my sin.3 For I acknowledge my transgressions: and my sin is ever before me.4 Against thee, thee only, have I sinned, and done this evil in thy sight: that thou mightiest be justified when thou speakest, and be clear when thou judgest.5 Behold, I was shapen in iniquity; and in sin did my mother conceive me.6 Behold, thou desirest truth in the inward parts: and in the hidden part thou shalt make me to know wisdom.7 Purge me with hyssop, and I shall be clean: wash me, and I shall be whiter than snow.8 Make me to hear joy and gladness; that the bones which thou hast broken may rejoice.9 Hide thy face from my sins, and blot out all mine iniquities. 10 Create in me a clean heart, O God; and renew a right spirit within me.11 Cast me not away from thy presence; and take not thy holy spirit from me.12 Restore unto me the joy of thy salvation; and uphold me with thy free spirit. 13 Then will I teach transgressors thy ways; and sinners shall be converted unto thee."

I knew from this passage alone, the process had to take place to get ME out of the way. There had to be a self-sacrificial ceremony, a washing and a purging of the lies I've embraced about Me. There had to be a deliverance from the mindset and a demolishing of the walls of strongholds that have been built up over time. There had to be an emptying of emotional baggage that I've carried around. The mask and the makeup had to come off, the plastered smile with the warm welcome wave from a wounded and weary soul immediately shifted to my hands lifted up in an act of surrender. I was tired of welcoming what I didn't want in my life or what I didn't deserve, even still not knowing my worth. I just knew there was something about me that I had not known before. I had to face the real music, which was me and the truth about me. All of these things had to be dealt with as verse 6 in Psalms 51 states in our scripture above, "Behold thou desires truth in the inward parts."

God deals with us in ever-deepening ways. Down, down, down, to the core, He goes, until He touches bottom. He has to go right into the innermost being. When we allow Him to, every title, position, perception, belief, and status is null and void; nothing else matters. He is after truth in the inward parts, right down into the depths of our being. Why? Because truth is His nature, and if we are to become one with Him and partake of

His divine nature we have to be truthful inwardly. Yahushua, Jesus Christ, the second Person of the Godhead, called Himself the Truth - "I am... the truth." And coming into the truth of who we are, we have to be truthful about where we are. My truth at that time was very simple and honest, "Father I just want to be free from me."

If I were to speak improper English, I would scream "Yay!" with excitement and say "Me got it!" Yes, "Me got it"! The truth of His word made ME free from Me! This was a great start, although the other members (my will and mind) were still alive and well, just waiting on me. The day "me got it", I FELT (as my emotion happily expressed) that it was now time for me to have a little talk with myself.

6

MYSELF – THE SELL OUT

Lord, I give myself to you; my God, I trust you.

Psalms 25:1-2

I am glad you have decided to take this road trip with me. It is my pleasure to share this part of my journey with you. Although I am still on my road to destiny, it is good for me to look into the rear view mirror and see how far I've come. I can now finally enjoy the journey and the beautiful view out of my window even while traveling in unknown territories. Only God knows what is ahead as I travel, but the great thing is as that He prepares me for the storms of life. Psalms 121:7 encourages me, "The LORD shall preserve thee from all evil: He will shall preserve thy soul." He will let nothing sneak up on the righteous; so in the meantime I am enjoying His beautiful creation, and understanding the importance of the seasonal changes in my life.

One of my favorite scriptures is found in Ecclesiastes 3:1-8, "To everything there is a season, and a time to every purpose under the heaven:2 A time to be born, and a time to die; a time to plant, and a time to pluck up that which is planted;3 A time to kill, and a time to heal; a time to break down, and a time to build up;4 A time to weep, and a time to laugh; a time to mourn, and a time to dance;5 A time to cast away stones, and a time to gather stones together; a time to embrace, and a time to refrain from embracing;6 A time to get, and a time to lose; a time to keep, and a time to cast away;7 A time to rend, and a time to sew; a time to keep silence, and a time to speak;8 A time to love, and a time to hate; a time of war, and a time of peace."

While on my journey there were many times I questioned God and His timing for certain seasons that I had to endure. Just when I thought I was traveling on Easy/Narrow Street, I was jolted multiple potholes that were there to slow me down. But as His spirit led me to this scripture, I was reminded anew that seasons do come and go, whether we like it or not. The seasonal changes are ultimately for our good. I'm sure this would explain some things that may have taken place in your life. Those things that you had no control over; you may have even questioned God about it when trying to resolve it yourself failed. Theologian John Wesley's notes and commentary defines a season as: "A season- A certain time appointed by God for its being and continuance, which no human wit or providence can alter". In other words, God has the right to change the course or direction of our lives for further development and growth anytime, any-where and for any reason that He wants to; without our consent or per-mission and there's nothing you or anyone can do about God's appointed time. We have to simply yield to the process and ask Him to reveal what it is you need to get out of that season. Embrace the seasons of life, it may not always feel right, but I guarantee that in His time you will experience a greater knowledge and clarity to weathering the storm. The scripture goes on to say "and a time to every purpose under heaven". As you continue to read this passage it gives you set times for every season that you will one day come to experience both spiritually and naturally. I could never understand the spiritual aspect of it, in fact I looked through the lenses of a victim, it seemed like I was in the season of breakdown all the time (verse 3). My famous line was the devil is always trying to attack me. Until I gained an understanding and realized and accepted that when you are in alignment with the will, plan and purpose of the Father - it is His do-ing. He is in control. This is all for purpose. I had to realize the time for breaking down, would bow to a time for building up. There were some mental strongholds that needed to be broken, belief systems destroyed, and there were soul ties that needed to be severed before the building. Every experience was tied in to my seasons for everything and time for purpose.

We have purpose while here on earth, each one of us! God had it in mind before the foundation of the world, He knew you and what you were to do here in the earth for His Glory. Do you know some people go to the grave never fulfilling purpose because they let what they did or what they've been through in Chrono's (chronological) "time" overshadow the true purpose of their existence? They were chasing dreams, without realizing purpose first. Some have traveled the same road in time searching for purpose –which they never found. How sad, God does not want this for His children. That's why it is imperative to find out what season and time you are in. God's timing for your purpose is best, anytime you move before time you take the risk of getting out the synch with Him. Never rush God's timing because you feel you are wasting it, because the process is necessary for you-- it is part of your purpose, and remember God is the redeemer of time and what is meant for you, will come in its season and time.

It looks like it's getting a little dark and cloudy out here. While I was not aware of the weather report calling for thunderstorms, there they were – looming and without notice. Do you see the clouds gathering in your life? I share this with you because I do not want you to be discouraged when you look out of your window and see thunderstorms, dark clouds and rainy days. Trust me, I have had many and still have them as I travel. This is the road that I came to terms with ME. I had to take control of myself, and come to grips with myself.

I recall traveling this road alone. I remember crying, and complaining. I would feel afraid when the night fell on this lonely road. I would be unsure of what would happen to me. It was this very place - where we are right now - that I started to feel uneasy. It was and it is an unfamiliar place. It was the first time that I had to take a deep breath and look within myself and figure things out. I felt turmoil within, the struggle within myself was present. I remember thinking: do I want to change? Or, should I just turn around and go back? I had to pull through, press through, (that strong will of mine), and talk myself into forward moving, to keep going. I convinced myself that I was getting closer to the destination. And, even though I still felt a little lost, I did not want to sell ME out. I cried, I screamed, "God help me!" Finally, I felt the release to continue on the road. Instantly fear left me and for the first time I felt a sense of connection with Myself. It took ME to humble Myself and give myself to Him and trust that He would now lead me and guide me!

Myself as it relates to the will, is the sellout of the three. You may have heard before when someone betrays another for their personal advancement they are a sell-out. Well that is how we look at "Myself" as it relates to the will. You would think that myself would go follow along with ME (emotions), and in most cases the two are like two peas in a pod; they will join forces, however the will could be a bit stubborn at time. Let's look at the will a little closer. According to the dictionary, generally, is that faculty of the mind which selects, at the moment of decision, the strongest desire from among the various desires present. It enables a person to act deliberately.

Will does not refer to any particular desire, but rather to the capacity to act decisively on one's desires. Within philosophy, the will is important as one of the distinct parts of the mind, along with reason and understanding. It takes your will to control self and to discipline self. If you are not willing, then you will not put the effort into doing anything outside of your will.

Now, let me explain the function of myself when we were in school we learned that it is used as an intensive of me or I. It intensifies who we are-- if Me is the show out, then Myself sells out to what Me portrays. In other words, myself identifies and puts a physical presence to what Me wants. I know it may be a bit confusing, but hang in here. I do understand in which the correct tense of these words should go but for the sake of the breakdown of Me, Myself and I - roll with me. I am taking an English class (during the writing of this book), which is why this is still fresh on my mind.

My is a possessive adjective- which are always placed before the noun that they modify. So in the example in which we are using me, myself and I ... SELF is being modified so that we identify who is at work. Self in action; and what is self? Self is the complete and essential being of a person; or a person's interest, advantage or welfare.

That's where selfishness comes in, as do self-satisfaction, self-reliance, and self-righteousness. You get the picture, right? The will and the self, working together, are definitely in need of the power of God to break them down. When God does it, what a humbling experience. The rollercoaster of emotions is now at rest and the ride is over. You can finally allow God to take control of the wheel.

The road in which we are traveling on right now, is the road of rebuilding. As I have shared MY experience with you, and what I felt as it started out, (which was a bit shaky and uncertain) it became clear to me that this route was necessary for travel. Although it was a long, dark and wintery back road which very few travel on, the Father revealed to me it was the road to the innermost part of my soul, and only He could navigate through it. I still had to be willing to let Him lead and go with Him.

Let me ask you a question? Have you ever given someone your soul completely? Your mind, your will and your emotions? And if so, how did they treat your soul? What did you learn from giving your all to someone? Did they care for your soul? Earlier we focused on the lyrics from a song by Beyoncé. The only conclusion she came to after enduring some things in a relationship was that he left her to deal with herself. (Me, myself and I). How can one rely on themselves when they're empty and broken? How could he have left her like that? A better question, how could someone do that to you? Life does not warn us or prepare us for seasonal changes.

Oh, my friend there is so much more to share.

I know you have given yourself to people or relationships who have either let you down or have attempted to break you down, until your soul either became bitter and wounded, or until you lost yourself in that dark place. God wants to restore your soul - every last piece of it. He wants the best for you, and has the best for you! What you have experienced up to this point is part of your purpose. Do not regret or devalue your experiences. Evaluate and learn from them. Step out of your SELF and look from His perspective. Use what you have learned to help someone else and use the experiences as building blocks. Let your breakdowns be your breakouts from selfishness and self-sabotage and become selfless; giving of yourself for a greater use, for His glory!

This season of rebuilding will require a stripping of Self, and it's nothing to fear because He does it in two ways, gently and loving; and the best part of it all is that He does not leave you empty and broken but He fills you with peace, hope and a joy that is indescribable. He replaces and restores abundantly.

It's a new season, it's a new day! This dreary road will not last always. The Father can change seasons as He chooses, remember He is control. The best part about it is - with the keys of understanding and faith - you can navigate through any kind of weather.

Well now, let's thank God for bringing us through the storm, it looks like it has passed us by.

We are headed in the right direction. I-777 is just ahead and we'll be there before you know it.

What a great accomplishment for me to reflect on this journey and know that this is where I came to terms with myself, by breaking the strong will of independence and submitting to the authority of the Spirit of the Most High. Not totally complete, but closer than ever, definitely in the right direction.

7

I – SOUL'D OUT

Hear, O Israel: The Lord our God is one Lord. And thou shalt love the Lord thy God, with all thine heart, with all thine soul, and with all thy might.

Deuteronomy 6:4-5

How do you feel? Take a deep breath, breathe in, and breathe out. I told you the storm would pass and seasons do change. In fact, it looks as if it never rained, right? Kind of reminds me of the weather in Texas. What beautiful rays of sun are beaming on us. Oh, by the way, if it is too bright for you, I have an extra pair of sunglasses for your use or please feel free to adjust your visor. I love the brightness of the sun; there is something about it that gives me a sense of knowing God is smiling on me. I love to take it all in. I have not always enjoyed it; especially during a very rough time that I went through years ago. I recall during one of my wintery moments, it was a cold, long, dreary period of complete darkness. I completely shut-down, closed my blinds and only did what was necessary outside of my house. It was so bad, that something as simple as opening my blinds were one of the hardest things for me to do. I stayed in this condition for longer than I should have and had become so use to darkness and pain, that light became a distraction to my disorder. I was defeated, and without hope. One morning I was awakened in my sleep about 4:00 am. I got out of the bed and went into the kitchen to get something to drink. I couldn't quite figure out why I got up, so I tried to find something to do since I would be getting up soon for work anyway. As I looked in the refrigerator I found something to snack on and drink and went to sit on my couch. I grabbed the remote and before I could turn on the television I sensed a strong impression to walk to the balcony and open the blinds, and so I did. I slowly walked over, peaked behind the blind and then unlocked, opened and stepped out on the balcony it was still dark, very still and nothing but silence. I looked up and saw the moon shining in the dark sky, and God spoke to my heart and said "Nicole, in your darkness I'm still your light." In that moment I wept and released so much pain. I believe deliverance from depression happened that early morning from a small act of obedience - simply opening my blinds and seeing Him in the midst of my darkness. From then until this very day, the first thing I do when I get out of the bed is open my blinds. It took some time for my family to get used to it especially during the early hours of the morning 4:00 a.m. or 5:00 a.m. But it's okay, as long as I am happy, they don't question the correlation between my peace and the blinds. That was a moment of revelation. I appreciate the light and this is why I love taking it all in, so that I can give light to others such as yourself. Let the sun shine on us and resonate in us as we ride into the light- take Him in, He is shining in every area of the soul!

What a journey so far! The GPS has confirmed we are not far from our destination. We have made it to the interstate which will lead us directly to where we need to be. The saying is true, funny how time flies when you are having fun. I know time is nearing for us to go our separate ways but I must admit-this has been fun for me. I love road trips especially when they are fruitful. I trust that every seed planted will flourish from and in your soul. I shared many things on the way, and I pray since you've made the decision to ride and listen to me that you heard God speak through me directly to your spirit and your soul. I would like for you to take heed to the scripture found in Isaiah 55:3, "Incline your ear, and come unto me: hear and your soul shall live and I will make an everlasting covenant with you that your soul shall live and I will make a covenant with you, even the sure mercies of David. KJV

This is my prayer for you; because you have inclined your ear and have come unto Him, all that He has for you will manifest in your life through this covenant!

GPS states we are on "I"-777 while we are traveling on interstate 777, let's recap and summarize from previous chapters: Me is who we embrace, (the show-off) myself is the one identical with me used reflexively; the sellout, whatever I will to do—guess what, I will do it. (It's my normal healthy state or condition) and lastly, we are left to conclude our conversation with the topic of "I". We have not talked much about I until now because it is the most important factor of the combo. I is who I have made up my mind to believe what I am and who I am. It is a reflection of the state of mind and the collection of thoughts that have been embraced and embedded over time. I'd like to use this example, if you've ever looked at the movie The Wizard of Oz, or the Wiz just think about the Wizard who hid behind the loud voice, the big mask and the one who was in complete control dictating while out of sight all that would take place in the lives of those he controlled; so it is with the "I". I is the member of the soul that sets precedence of our reality, our environment and ultimately our life, so let's put it like this and oh excuse the improper English again this time I am stated it in sentence form in hopes it makes it a little easier, here it goes, I tells me what to do, and myself locks in and puts an action to it.

I must put state this DISCLAIMER: I am in no way stating you have three different personalities, however, if you find that there is another person you frequently speak of in identifying yourself with, this book only scratches the surface. Let it be as an introduction to bring awareness to a potential condition that needs to be treated. It could be that there are some deep rooted issues that need to be worked through by way of psychological and spiritual counseling and deliverance. I recommend to get immediate help. In contrast, the overall message in this book is to bring consciousness to know who you really are and to have a sound mind, a peaceful soul and a willing spirit to defy the selfish desires of your soul that could potentially cause your soul to be out of alignment. This is also a reminder that it is imperative for your soul to prosper for healthy and wealthy living. It is equally important and a must for you to continuously work out the issues of your soul, with that being said let's talk about I.

Yes, the little yet big I, the puffed up yet weak one, the one that seems to lead by its own set of rules, the I who is behind all of the façade, the one who is ultimately in control of me and myself, the one who is responsible for what comes into the soul. The one who introduced you to you! The big I, is the master mind behind it all.

We've heard the very popular statement that the mind is a terrible thing to waste. The mind is a part of the soul and if the mind is not functioning in alignment with the will and emotions then there is a separation. Sometimes you will hear people say I've lost my mind, or I must be out of my mind. There are just saying that somewhere down the line there has been a detachment, the dysfunction between the three are not sync to make sound decisions. When there is separation amongst the three it keeps us from connecting from our true identity.

How did this happen? I'm sure you're wondering. Well, I believe in some cases, somewhere down the line whether in the birth canal or as a child --circumstances or experience has caused the real you to hide behind the shadows fearing exposure to the light! Light is always there to expose every dark thing. The enemy loves to work in the dark. If he can get you to believe whatever lie he suggest, whatever lie that he used someone to speak over your life, whatever he has HEARD you say out of your own mouth against yourself, he will strategize until you embrace, give in and believe! He will pursue until he wins. Well my friend, it is not so, the battle is over as of today. The Father has sent me to break down barriers in your life, He has sent with a soul bondage breaking message too free you from yourself! It is time to deal with I. This one letter word has done more damage than the word and meaning for damage itself. I have and is stopping you from succeeding, simply because you have not fully embraced who you are. Just ponder this for a moment, and think about your words-- more times than less what you release out of your mouth daily are words that kill your esteem, that talk you out of greatness; words such as: I can't do this, I can't figure it out, I don't understand, I am not good enough, I don't know why,

I hate my life, I don't like my body, etc. the list goes on. How many times have we self-inflicted or spoken to ourselves with negative words? Nine times out of ten we are not building our I's up, we are constantly competing, comparing and compromising who we are and who others think that we are. Instead of taking the time to build we tear ourselves to shreds. Okay, so let me speak for myself, you may or may not be able to relate and this may not be your story however, I wish someone would have told me long ago. I have wasted part of my life trying to meet others expectations, standards and cultural cliques, because I was like the woman in Lisa Stansfield's song we talked about previously, I've been around the world meaning relationships, friendships, family ships, looking for my baby... that part of my soul that needed to be nurtured, loved, and developed. I was looking outside of God for external love and affection from someone who couldn't meet the internal need. If you recall the chorus of the same song, she said, as if she were stuttering but she identified the problem she said it three times, "I, I, I, I can't find my baby" she was on to something, but didn't quite figure it out she put more of the focus on looking for her baby. Many of us have done this over time, we've blamed others without taking a good look at I, I, I,

You may be wondering why I didn't start with I first. I'll tell you why. I believe because His ways are not our ways, He does things differently than we would. There is no exact formula to how God does things, every drawing to Himself or reconciling to Himself is different and it takes different circumstances and different approaches to draw people. However, I've seen it happen over and over again, sometimes a great way to get someone's attention is when you hurt their ego, or when you take something that they have deemed as a god in their life, there are other ways that God will get the attention of His people. Some of us will get it, some of us won't. Sometimes others will blame everyone else and stay bitter, then there are some who will eventually catch on and turn inward and start evaluating, questioning and sometimes blame themselves or take responsibility. Let's go back to the first song from Beyoncé', the first verse written: "I can't believe I believed everything we had would last... silly of me. What happened here in the song, is that her ego was deflated. She fell for a man, who eventually showed her that he did not respect her. The image, the ego, the ME that had been presented to the world on the outside was now in jeopardy of being exposed and embarrassed, and she couldn't believe that it was happening to her. Have you ever reacted this way? How did you deal with embarrassment? How did you deal with your hurt? Did you take an evaluation of yourself or did you focus your attention on the behavior of the other person or how it left you? As we learn from the lyrics of the song, instead of dealing with it she remained in the same condition. Instead of finding out why she (I) believed what she believed in the first place, instead of taking the time to find out about her belief system, if there was a sign of weakness for attracting such a man, did she compromise somewhere when allowing him into her life? Were there signs? What was he attracted to? There are many ways to analyze the decision she made in the first place. But instead she shook it off, built a wall of protection and hid herself within herself. It's not a good place to park, especially when you're not sure what awaits.

As God deals with us, I believe He has to break through the exterior, and deal first with who we have created, (me) and then break the will (myself) which is necessary before one would even be open to looking within for the truth.

When God has total access to our natural, He then adds His super, which makes our encounters supernatural, which supersedes our expectations.

Let me briefly share three accounts in the Bible where a supernatural encounter with God took place. Each one of my examples had come face to face with I. They faced the truth about who they were, what stagnated them and what they believed about themselves.

Exodus chapters two and three begin with the story of Israel descendants in Egypt. If you don't know the story of Moses read it when you can in its entirety. I will paraphrase. Chapter two gives reference to The Pharaoh of Egypt and his order to kill all of the Hebrew boys and save the girls. Moses was just a baby and his mother hid him for as long as she could to keep him safe and to prevent his death. When she could not hide him anymore she made a basket, put him in it, and took him to the river to save his life. As Moses' little sister watched from afar she noticed that Pharaoh's Egyptian daughter, (who went out to bathe in the same river) saw the basket drew him out. She took him to the palace, cared for and raised him. As Moses grew, he knew that He was not a true Egyptian. He knew despite all of the privileges he had, the fine clothes he wore, and his status as the Prince of Egypt - it wasn't who he really was.

I would even say that his position was not even enough to compromise the truth in his heart. It was his circumstance as a baby and his upbringing that allowed him to be in the position he was in; however, it still did not take the place of purpose for His life. It wasn't until one day he saw an Egyptian soldier beating a Hebrew slave that Moses had to make a decision to follow through with what he knew in his heart was wrong treatment for his people. He quickly came to terms with himself and made a decision to kill the Egyptian. The next day Moses fled Egypt. This began his long and wintery road process. I am sure he had much time to work through his emotions until he was out of his feelings about what took place before he fled from Egypt. I'm sure he had come to terms about his past life with himself on the lonely road before meeting his wife. What he hadn't done was come to the fullness of who he was, he was not quite sure or confident of his identity. Before Moses did all of the great things he did for the children of Israel, he had some issues to deal with. Skipping forward, (please stay with me), we find Moses at the mountain of God called Horeb or Mt. Sinai – at the burning bush. By this time, he had escaped ME. He really didn't have much to prove. He didn't have the clothing of a prince, or the accolades or authority to prove to anyone, so he made the decision to just exist. His philosophy became this is just me, like me or leave me. So with ME's attitude, Myself made the decision to start a new life. I believe it is in Chapter 3 verse 2 and on Moses comes face to face with I. After the initial conversation with God and receiving an overview of what God wanted him to do for the children of Israel. Moses response (in verse 11) was a question, "Who am I"?

What a profound question. Have you ever asked this question to yourself or to God? How appropriate to be in the presence of God and ask Him, who am I? The prince of Egypt was asking - who am I? He was popular amongst the Egyptians. He was somebody! But he was standing before the Almighty God with nothing, no title, no power asking God who am I.

Anytime you invest in the presence of God, all of the hidden things that you have buried will be exposed. This is the time that all you have believed that was contrary to who God said you were will be brought to the light. Moses began to pour out his insecurities. Chapter 4:10 (paraphrasing), he told God I am not a man with eloquent speech and slow of tongue. He had a stuttering problem and did not feel adequate enough to talk to a guy like Pharaoh on behalf of the God of Israel. After the dialogue he and the Father had, he still couldn't see himself the way God did. Why? Because he became one with what he thought of himself... the mind embraced a suggestive thought of the enemy of who he was not and Moses fell for it and believed so he could only see from that perspective. The bible says that faith cometh by hearing - so he heard himself over and over - I can't speak fluently, I stutter and other repetitive thinking led to this disbelief.

God had to take a different approach with Moses. He chose Moses for a work but had to work with him and through him. But despite his low self- esteem and confidence, God saw differently, he was the man for the job! This is what He wants you to see, that there is much more to you when you align yourself to His thoughts. He needs all of you, just like he needed all of Moses. He knew what Moses lacked and it was confidence. Moses, realized early on that he was different than the other Egyptians, he left the culture of wickedness. He came to grips with himself and settled with his decision. Fast forward, he fell in love and worked to meet his daily needs living a normal life. I believe Moses had not yet realized his full potential or purpose until He dealt with I... I was in his way. He was worried about himself and his performance whether he would be good enough, and he also worried about the people and what they would think or say. I believe he was vulnerable because he had never been propositioned into presenting the real him, all he knew was to fill the role of a prince.

God became angry with Moses not because he lacked confidence but he didn't trust the I AM, but God took the time to reassure him of who

He was. When Moses complained about his stuttering problem in verse 11 and 12, God eliminated the excuse. He told him that He would be his mouth and would show him what to say and do. He said tell the children of Israel that the I Am is sending you. Moses despite his challenges, went. Moses was special, after all God spoke to Him, and assured Him that He would give him all that he needed for the assignment. Listen to this, just two chapters later Moses comes back with a similar response questioning his existence. He said, God I heard all of that you said, about who you are, but again who am I that Pharaoh would hear from uncircumcised lips. Ha! Can you believe it? Yes, I can, I've done it before. God has given me assignments to do but I did not feel worthy, capable or confident. Over time, I've learned that confidence is only gained the more you spend time with Him.

When you humbly submit yourself to God the "Big I "in your life diminishes and God is able to use you to fulfill purpose all the while revealing Himself to you so that you can see who you are in Him!

Another example is found in Isaiah chapter 6. In contrast to Moses' title stripped before his encounter, Isaiah had already been a prophet of God, he was already in position and in purpose. He had visions about Judah and Jerusalem and he was conveying the messages of the Lord. In chapter 6, he gives an account of his vision of the Lord; he saw the Lord high and lifted up., He saw Seraphim angels declaring, "Holy, holy, holy." Could you imagine having such an encounter as Isaiah did? But this encounter revealed a truth that Isaiah had to admit to in verse 5, he said "Woe is me? For I am a man undone; because I am a man of unclean lips, and I dwell in the midst of a people of unclean lips; for mine eyes have seen the King, the Lord of host."

Isaiah was humbled in the presence of God and desired to be pure and clean after the new insight of himself and those around him as being undone and with unclean lips. The glorious light shone on his soul. Although he was a prophet of God, in order to represent authentically, his words had to align themselves with the word of the Lord and it began with a cleansing of the heart. As soon as Isaiah got a revelation the angel came and touched his lips.

I know this seems like much, but I feel that I need to share this with you so you are no longer ashamed of whatever is stopping you. I don't know what your current position is in this life or what you do for God; but to be sent by God is impossible to do it in your own power. The I has to be removed. Later in the scripture God asked a question; "whom shall I send" and who will go for us? There was nobody else in the room that he could be referring but Isaiah's response was, "Here am I!"

I love the way he phrased his words, some would say here I am Lord send me, but he said here am I, that small detail expresses Isaiah's humility. He knew he was a man undone and if Yahweh, God did not go before him, he would speak from unclean lips while prophesying representing God. Anyone commissioned by God should humbly submit with this thought in mind as God told Moses, tell them I am that I am, who will lead me, will watch over and cover me, will heal me and help me from insecurities, anxiety, fears, and temptations. We should always put the AM before the I because there is nothing within ourselves that can compare to the power of God that works within. I am only bold and confident in Him.

Lastly Jeremiah's calling was similar to Moses. In chapter one, verse six he said: "Then said I: ah, Lord God! I am a child." He did not feel that he was qualified enough, as if there were an age restriction. God had already told him that he knew him while he was in his mother's womb (verse 5). Then after Jeremiahs excuse, The Father responded to Jeremiah in verse 7; "Do not say you are a child, for you are going where I send and will speak what I say." He said a little more in scripture but what stood out to me was that God touched his mouth and said, "Behold I have put my words in your mouth." God is not concerned about your natural age or how long you've been in ministry. He is looking at your heart and if you are willing to submit yourself to His leading and guidance. In fact, I have seen where God will elevate someone (a babe in Christ) who desires righteousness and holiness rather than one who is seasoned but desires popularity and pleasure. There are no limits or restrictions in God!

Each account of these men were different in what caused their insecurities but what they all had in common was that they came to terms with what handicapped them for so long after encountering the presence of

God. Another thing that stuck out was after each of the discussions, The Father sealed what took place by touching, placing or filling their mouths/lips with His words. He knew a divine touch was necessary for them to restrict and limit what came from their mouths. They could not speak or feed on what they dealt with, such as lack of confidence, gossip, hypocrisy and intimidation. Praise God as their story unfolds and ends they were all successful in the assignment they were sent to do! Each encounter we spoke of and many others recorded in the Scriptures were life changing. They had an opportunity and privilege to realize His sovereignty, His love and His mercy. They saw Him as ONE LORD, and each one made a conscious decision to love Him according to Deuteronomy 6:4-5 with all thine heart, with all thy soul and with all thy might. In other words, their emotions, will and mind, (me, myself and I) were in synch under the power of His spirit. They were SOUL'd Out, to Him, His ways, and His will.

Without my encounter experience, I would not be here sharing with you today. Father revealed this to me over time and showed me that many people cannot get past their feelings, their thoughts or simply their strong wills because they just don't know who to trust outside of themselves. Yes, and I know this to be very true, because I was that girl, that woman in every example presented. However, He assured me that I could trust Him. It was not easy for me to simply trust in someone that I had never seen, but the more I searched for Him He revealed himself to me through scripture, through confirmations of my silent prayers (which He answered) and in many other ways. I turned the radio off, and forbid myself to hear another sad love song, or a song that kept the repetitive cycles happening. I had to put the brakes on in my life and sit in my car until I came to a place of stillness in my soul.

Psalms 131 says, "Surely, I have calmed and quieted my soul, like a weaned child with his mother; like a weaned child is my soul within me."

Not only did he heal and deliver ME but I kept hearing a melody in my spirit that soon connected to my soul as He rejoiced and sang songs of deliverance over me; according to Zephaniah 3:14-17, He gave me a new song to sing.

The song of hope, restoration and oneness is the song that I was commissioned to share with you. It was no coincidence, nor was it just a mere opportunity for you to decide to read this book and take the ride with me today, but it was by divine appointment. All of what you and I have faced, the internal conflict or torture within, in addition to life's challenges, rejection, abuse, hurt, betrayal pain and anything else that we face from time to time or repeatedly have now come to a head and have to be dealt with in order to reach the fullest potential and to walk worthy of the call on your life.

Let's face it, you have been your own ride or die far too long, and some have even died riding this journey without a soul mate. We have looked for others to mate our souls with but today God wants your soul! He wants a sincere cry out to be one with Him! We have picked up hitchhikers along the way. We have lost direction along the way, and we have driven the same roads for so long. We have lost the key of life, and some have gone from sojourners to wanderers, but one day no matter our journey, we will all come to a cliff or a dead end. The choice is yours. It's imperative to get off Self road. If you don't, you are driving further away from the truth and living an altered reality of me, myself and I.

Well this is it! We have made it! Look around, it's beautiful huh? Looks familiar right? I know what you're thinking. You must think I am crazy; all this time we've driven just to end up right back where we started from. I know, I know. It was necessary for you to take another route that was unfamiliar to you so that when you make the decision to follow the path, you will remember every stop we've made along the way; and you will identify what to do when you hit the long wintery road. You will remember each landmark and prayerfully this conversation will stay with you as encouragement to know that you have a sister who has test driven and found the road trip to be worth the ride!

My friend, this is where I leave you, (hugs) I love you with the Father's love, and pray for traveling grace and mercies. I thank you for spending time and chatting with me. Oh wait, one last thing, I want to give you a new cd for you to listen to while on your journey. In this song, I am proud to say He is The Author and The Finisher, He used me to write my journey and sing a new song entitled Me, Myself and I – One with You, I pray it will encourage and inspire you on your journey.

Until our paths meet again, may the Father's love, peace and blessings consume and flood your soul!

PRAYER

Let's pray,

Father, I pray for my friend. I pray that your angels will encamp all around them, and go before them to lead and guide them through the journey of their soul. We agree today as we both lift our soul to You that You will become the lover of our souls, we allow You full access to shine your light on every dark area to bring revelation, inspiration and motivation. Let us come into an awareness and greater understanding of Your hidden truths of who you are to us, and who we are to You. Father we repent of our stubbornness, independence, and any wickedness towards You, we pray that You forgive us, help us, as our soul desperately cries out to be one with You!

We are grateful and thankful for Your Holy Spirit that has spoken to our hearts through this book. Now we give ourselves to You, to set us apart to walk in Your spirit and live our lives pleasing to You. We love you with all of hearts, our souls, our minds and our strength!

In Yahushua, Jesus Christ name we pray,

Amen.

REFLECTIONS

The topic of SOUL'D OUT is one that we believers should become more concerned about in these last days. As soldiers, we should be winning souls for the Kingdom of God. Scripture even declares that he who wins souls is wise. With that said, I am grateful for the opportunity to write a book that has literally changed my own life, allowing me to gain deeper insight on and revelation of the SOUL. This process and journey has developed in me an ongoing practice of God's presence as well as a diligence in seeking Him for strategies and tools to combat the enemy of my soul. It has also heightened my awareness of how necessary it is to daily examine and empty my soul with the cleansing of the water of God's Word.

It is important for us to see the enemy as an assassin of the soul. Satan's main goal, job and assignment is to kill, steal and destroy. He has wiggled and enticed his way into our souls' homes. The keys are accessed by way of what we release from our mouths and what we accept as true and real in our minds.

The Bible declares in the Book of James, Chapter 3 that, in the last days, many will become lovers of themselves. It goes on to list other selfish and disobedient ways of this world, which we see even now. As this passage of scripture sets forth, nothing good comes from the flesh. Furthermore, it is the world that promotes self-love and pride. The enemy wants us to be so full of ourselves because he knows that anything which comes from "self" will not glory in the presence of the Most High. If we put anything--whether it be people, places, money, fame, cars, children and even me, myself and I--before Yahweh, then it's idolatry!

I have been asked, "Why would you use worldly songs to get your point across?" And my answer is, "Why not?" Believe it or not, media is one of the strongest weapons used by the enemy to keep saints and sinners alike stuck in a particular moment of time, state of emotion or mindset through the use of carefully-crafted subliminal messages. Even I—a Bible-believing saint, praise team leader, and church goer--was kept entangled in a web of emotions that prevented me from tapping into that intimate place of selfless worship for which I longed. If Satan can get the church listening to worldly songs, then it is up to us to meet the people of God where they are with an even more compelling message of hope, redemption and freedom.

In closing, it is my prayer that your soul has been touched and enlightened to the point that nothing will ever convince you to go backwards. I am grateful and humbled to share what Father has released me to share, as this message is relevant for the Body of Christ. It is a clarion call to come out of the flesh and into the spirit! This message serves as a wakeup call for the sleepers to awaken from their slumber and arise from their defeat! It is to bring awareness to the Body of Christ as well as all mankind to be careful of what we allow in our ear gates and eye gates, so that our souls will not be contaminated with ungodly influences but rather caressed with our Father's love!

ONE with Him!

Peace & Blessings,

Charese Nicole Matthews